Jesus and the Streets

The Loci of Causality for the Intra-Racial Gender Academic Achievement Gap in Black Urban America and the United Kingdom

Paul C. Mocombe,
Carol Tomlin,
and Victoria Showunmi

University Press of America,® Inc.
Lanham • Boulder • New York • Toronto • Plymouth, UK

Copyright © 2016 by University Press of America,® Inc.
4501 Forbes Boulevard, Suite 200, Lanham, Maryland 20706
UPA Acquisitions Department (301) 459-3366

Unit A, Whitacre Mews, 26-34 Stannary Street,
London SE11 4AB, United Kingdom

Library of Congress Control Number: 2015942210
ISBN: 978-0-7618-6619-0 (pbk : alk. paper)—ISBN: 978-0-7618-6620-6 (electronic)

∞™ The paper used in this publication meets the minimum requirements of American
National Standard for Information Sciences Permanence of Paper for Printed Library
Materials, ANSI/NISO Z39.48-1992.

Contents

Acknowledgments

This work, as with everything we pen,
is done in the name of the ancestors . . .

Introduction

The black male/female academic achievement gap is an empirical problematic that dates back to the late 1980s and early 1990s. Overwhelmingly, like all other groups in American and British societies, black females tend to significantly outperform black males on standardized tests, reading and writing in particular, giving rise to what is commonly referred to in the academic literature as the black intra-racial gender academic achievement gap between black boys and girls (Wright, 2013; Mocombe and Tomlin, 2013; Showunmi, 2013). Unlike white British and Americans, however, where boys typically tend to outperform girls in science and math, and girls tend to outperform boys in reading and writing. In the African American and black British Caribbean communities in the United States and United Kingdom, respectively, girls typically outperform boys in almost all areas, reading, writing, math, and science, of standardized testing leading to great social inequalities in the society and disidentification with school among black males (Ogbu, 1986; Steele, 1997, 1998; Wilson, 1998; Mocombe, 2005, 2008; Wright, 2013; Mocombe and Tomlin, 2013; Mocombe et al, 2013; Showunmi, 2013).

In the United States, the academic achievement reading proficiency rate of black males are twice as low as both white males and black females; the employment rate of black men aged 18 to 24 is 30 percent lower than that belonging to young men of other races or nationality; two-thirds of these black males do not attend college compared with approximately 60 percent of both white males and black females; black men make up 40 percent of all prison inmates, but less than 7 percent of the entire US population; and they are less likely to attend any form of religious institutions (Steele, 1997; Haskins, 2006; King, 2006; Hanson et al., 2007; Wilson, 2007; Mocombe and Tomlin, 2013). Conversely, black women constitute over 80 percent of the black church; the unemployment rate of black women is nearly 20 per-

1

cent less than that of black men while in the past three decades the annual mean income of black women has nearly equaled that of black men; black women enroll in college at the same rate as white males and graduate at twice the rate of black men; black women earn 63 percent and 71 percent respectively the number of graduate and professional degrees awarded to all African- Americans (King, 2006; Parker and Orozco, 2008; Cross, 2009).

Similarly in the United Kingdom, the academic achievement rate of black British males on the General Certificate of Secondary Education (GCSE) are twice as low as both white males and black females; black British men aged 16-24 years of age have the highest rates of unemployment, 48 percent, than any other group; black British women are more likely to be employed, 67 percent of the British Labor Market, and earn twice as much as black men; black British Caribbean men 18-24 are overwhelmingly represented in the British prison system vis-à-vis their general population; lastly, black British women constitute over 80 percent of all black church-goers in black British communities (Peach, 1996; Berthoud, 2009; Mocombe and Tomlin, 2013).

As these statistics demonstrate black females, in both the US and UK, are more likely to attend church, be academically successful, educated, and employed, than their black male counterparts who overwhelmingly are unemployed, associated with athletics, the urban street life, and criminalized in the two societies. In this work, we posit the protestant capitalist social structure of class inequality and its ideological apparatuses, the black church, education, media, prisons, and the streets, in black communities in the US and UK as the background for "enframing," conceptualizing, and exploring the black/white academic achievement gap in general and this intra-racial gender achievement gap between black boys and girls in particular over John Ogbu's cultural-ecological model and Claude Steele's disidentification thesis.

Ostensibly, two dominant theories attempt to explain the gender academic achievement gap, and its social ramifications, as it pertains to all ethnic and racial groups. First, researchers typically highlight the neurological and psychological maturation of girls over boys. That is, the differing maturation speed of the brain between boys and girls affects how each gender processes information and how they perform on standardized tests. Girls mature faster and typically perform better on standardized tests early on in their academic careers; however, boys tend to catch up and perform better in their adolescent years especially in science and math (Hanlon, Thatcher, and Cline, 1999; Sax, 2005). Second, other researchers point to social roles and gender socialization (Good, 1987; Wilson, 1998; Jencks and Phillips, 1998; Tach and Farkas, 2006). Girls are more likely to do well in subject areas, reading and writing, that are deemed more feminine and boys tend to do better in areas, math and science, that are deemed more masculine. This is a product of gender socialization over any sort of biological determinism.

In terms of African American and black British Caribbean black males and females in the United States and United Kingdom, respectively, the socialization hypothesis has dominated the social science literature over the past four decades (Wilson, 1998; Jencks and Phillips, 1998; Wright, 2013; Mocombe et al, 2013). In this work, we assess the socialization hypothesis and offer an alternative framework to better explain the aforementioned statistics and academic underachievement phenomenon among blacks in both the UK and US. In opposition to John Ogbu's burden of acting white hypothesis and Claude Steele's disidentification theory, we posit a structural Marxian hermeneutical framework, Paul C. Mocombe's (Mocombe, 2005, 2008, 2009; Mocombe and Tomlin, 2010, 2013) "mismatch of linguistic structure and social class function" hypothesis, as a more appropriate hermeneutical (socialization) framework for framing, conceptualizing, and exploring the black/white academic achievement gap in general and the black male/ black female intra-racial academic achievement gap in particular. This structural Marxian hermeneutical framework posits the protestant capitalist social structure of class inequality, mode of production, and its ideological apparatuses, the black church, education, media, and the streets, in black communities in the US and UK as the background for "enframing," conceptualizing, and exploring the black/white academic achievement gap in general and the intra-racial gender gap in particular.

BACKGROUND OF THE PROBLEM

Contemporarily, social scientists appropriate two dominant socialization theories to contextualize, conceptualize, and explain the black male/female intra-racial gender social and academic achievement gap, John Ogbu's (1986) burden of acting white or oppositional culture hypothesis and Claude Steele's (1997) stereotype threat theory. Ogbu's and Steele's positions are broader theories that attempt to explain the black/white academic achievement gap in general. The black/white academic achievement gap is a product of black socialization within marginalized and discriminated against black social groups, which causes them to disparage academic achievement or disidentify with school either for fear of confirming white stereotypes regarding black intellectual inferiority, a la Claude Steele, or for fear of being labeled white by their black peers, a la John Ogbu. As these theories pertain to the black male/female academic achievement gap, both positions posit that the black male/female intra-racial gender academic achievement gap is a product of disidentification with school amongst black males as opposed to black females who are more likely to achieve academically over their male counterparts (Wilson, 1998).

Traditional environmental theories, building on the cultural-ecological approach of John Ogbu, posits that black American students, given their racial marginalization within the socioeconomic social structure of American capitalist society, either developed an oppositional social "identity-in-differential" that defined "certain activities, events, symbols, and meanings as not appropriate for them because those behaviors, events, symbols, and meanings are characteristic of white Americans" (Fordham and Ogbu 1986, pg. 181), or that such an "underclass" identity stemmed from a "culture of poverty" that devalued educational attainment (Jencks and Phillips, 1998, pg. 10). This thesis has come to be known in the social science literature as the oppositional culture thesis (Gordon, 2006; Tyson et al, 2005; Ainsworth-Darnell and Downey, 1998, 2002; Cook and Ludwig 1998; Wilson, 1998; Farkas et al, 2002; Steele, 1997; Ogbu, 1991). Both positions, essentially, argue that the choice between exercising a black cultural ethos and striving for academic success within the larger society diametrically oppose one another. Further goes the argument, this conflict contributes to underachievement among black adolescent students vis-à-vis their white counterparts who do not encounter this cultural opposition. Black students intentionally underachieve for fear of being labeled "acting white" by their black adolescent peers who view academic achievement and success as the status marker of whites.

For Fordham and Ogbu the "burden of acting white," among black Americans is a constant phenomenon throughout the United States, which among black school children has come to be used as a larger oppositional peer culture with respect to indicators of academic performance and success (Fordham and Ogbu, 1986, pg. 181). That is to say, as Tyson et al points out, "academic achievement is not valued in the community because it is perceived as conforming to standard norms of success among white Americans" (Tyson et al, 2005, pg. 584). This position is complimented by the broader conservative hypothesis, the culture-of-poverty position, which posits that impoverished black Americans, the "black underclass," as a cultural community devalue education, "the protestant work ethic," and the two-parent family in favor of instant gratification and episodic violence, which gives rise to the larger oppositional peer culture prevalent among adolescent school aged children (Steele, 1990, pgs. 95-96; Steele, 1992, pg. 75). Within this oppositional cultural understanding, black males academically underachieve vis-à-vis their female counterparts because they view academic success as the status marker of white males and females, and disidentify with achieving academically and socially for fear of being labeled white or effeminate, respectively, by their black male peers. Instead they are more likely to identify with black non-dominant cultural capital, speaking Black/African American English Vernacular (BEV/AAEV), athletics, playing the class clown, hip-hop culture, and the street life where they achieve their status in the larger society (Ogbu, 1986; Wilson, 1998; Carter, 2005; Mocombe and Tomlin, 2010, 2013).

Numerous scholars in the United Kingdom have extrapolated Ogbu's theory to black British Caribbean pupils (Wright, 2013; Mocombe and Tomlin, 2010, 2013). That is, black British youth, males in particular, view academic success and education as the status marker of women and white British society. As a result, they are less likely to apply themselves academically for fear of being labeled "acting white" by their black British male peers (Mocombe and Tomlin, 2010, 2013).

Whereas in the socialization of blacks in the larger mainstream society, Ogbu focuses on racial identification, blacks view academic success as the status marker of whites, as the locus of causality for black disidentification with school, Claude Steele focuses on self-esteem and racial stereotype threats. Similarly to Ogbu's hypothesis, Steele's (1997) stereotype threat theory posits that blacks underachieve vis-à-vis their white counterparts for fear of confirming the negative racial stereotypes whites associate with their intellectual abilities, and the threat that poses to their self-esteem. In other words, blacks do not place much effort on standardized tests for fear of confirming white stereotypes of their intellectual abilities when they do not do well, and this subsequently affects their feeling of well-being and racial pride. Within this understanding, black males predominantly disidentify or disconnect with school for fear of confirming black intellectual inferiority, and the threat that fear poses to their self-esteem and racial identity. The coping strategy implemented by the group at risk for being stereotyped is to disidentify with the domain that poses the threat. In the case of academic achievement, this domain would be school (Steele, 1997). School identification is the central component of stereotype threat theory (Steele, 1998). As a result of their lack of success in school and fear of confirming white stereotypes associated with their lack of success, black males are more likely to disidentify with school as opposed to black females who tend to be more academically sound and successful.

CRITIQUE OF OGBU AND STEELE

In the use of Ogbu's and Steele's positions to account for the intra-racial gender academic achievement gap, black socialization is seen as either determined by whites or their black peers as the locus of causality for black male academic underachievement vis-à-vis whites in general and their black female counterparts in particular. For the most part, researchers have found very little empirical evidence to support Ogbu's oppositional culture hypothesis as either the locus of causality for the black/white academic achievement gap, or the disidentification with school found among black males (Wilson,

1998; Carter, 2003, 2005). Instead some opportunity gap scholars in the likes of Prudence Carter (2003, 2005) interpret the hypothesis as a real struggle inner-city African American youth face between pursuing the dominant cultural capital of the larger American society at the expense of their non-dominant cultural capital of their inner-city communities, which highlights other activities, athletics, hip-hop culture, speaking Black/African-American English, and the street life as status markers.

We agree with Carter on this non-dominant cultural capital identification with (black underclass) identity as a more appropriate interpretation of Ogbu's thesis. However, we disagree with her opportunity gap conclusions and Bourdieuian cultural interpretation. We see the struggle from a structural as opposed to a postmodern Bourdieuian cultural capital perspective highlighted by Prudence Carter. That is, the conflict as we interpret the opposition found among inner-city African American and black British Caribbean youth is not between different forms of cultural capital. For us, Bourdieuian cultural capital is an account of class structural reproduction and differentiation in capitalist societies, not an account of alternative forms, outside of class structural reproduction and differentiation, of cultural practices arrived-at through the deferment of meaning in ego-centered communicative discourse as highlighted by Jacques Derrida's notion of *différance*. In other words, we are not suggesting African American and black British Caribbean youth have a differential cultural identity from their white counterparts. On the contrary, our argument here is that the divergences in practical consciousnesses between blacks and their white counterparts are a product of structural differentiation and not culture. As such, the conflict as we interpret the opposition found among inner-city African American and black British Caribbean youth is a relational problem between ideological apparatuses and social class roles fostered in black America and the United Kingdom by the larger societies' capitalist social structure of racial-class inequality, and not their cultural values, which is no different from white America and the United Kingdom, respectively. That is to say, historically speaking, the capitalist social structure of racial-class inequality as constituted via ideological apparatuses such as the black church, education, media, prisons, and the streets in both countries interpellated and structurally produced two distinct racial-classes, or social class language games, in black communities, i.e., a black middle class and an underclass centered on their social class roles in the societies. Their cultural worldviews, structured by the Protestant Ethic and the spirit of capitalism via ideological apparatuses such as the church, education, prisons, the streets, and hip-hop culture, is no different from their white counterparts. However, what is distinguishable between some blacks and their white counterparts are their class divisions/positions in ideological apparatuses and social relations to production not their cultural identities (Wilson, 1978). Church-attending and educated black middle class practices are more in line with that of their white middle class counterparts over the practices of the latter, black underclass, which are interpellated by different ideological apparatuses, i.e., the streets, prisons, etc. (Steele, 1997, 1998). However, the latter's practices are not cultural but structural. The black underclass tends to be less educated and poor, and as a result constitute material practices within ideological apparatuses, streets, prisons, and athletic and entertainment industries, which interpellate them around their poor material conditions within their urban (street) environments. These poor material practices, attending (or not) church, prison practices (sagging their pants, hustling, etc.), speaking Ebonics or Black British Talk, hustling and pimping, playing sports, and entertaining on the block, which are responses to structural practices, poor housing, schools, economic opportunities, despair, of the inner cities, and the ideological apparatuses, prisons, the streets, social welfare, after-school programs, sports, etc., in place to control and correct these practices, become cultural over generations and in the logic of Prudence Carter and other oppositional cultural theorists. However, the underlying ontology, the Protestant Ethic and the spirit of capitalism, among the black underclass is the same as in bourgeois black and white America, which seeks status, upward mobility, economic gain, etc. via the church, education, and professional roles over the street life, rapping, playing sports, the entertainment industry, etc., of the inner-cities.

As such, whereas Carter and many oppositional cultural theorists view the aforementioned structural opposition between blacks and whites as a conflict between different cultural capital and habitus in Bourdieuian parlance, we view Pierre Bourdieu's theory and its usage among scholars as a culturalization of capitalist racial-class structural reproduction and differentiation. As a result, we view the black/white academic achievement gap and the disidentification with school among black males in the US and UK as opposed to their female counterparts to be a product of their identification with the dominant social class roles, athletes, entertainers, and the street life, which do not require education or academic success, they as a racial-class group are over-represented as playing in the societies as opposed to the amount of capital they may or may not possess. This is a subtle difference between our position and the oppositional culture theory position. It is not that black males in both countries choose not to place effort on education as the means to achieving economic gain, status, and upward social mobility because of their culture which is no different from white Brits and Americans. Our position is that they choose, as Ogbu highlights, to identify with ideological apparatuses and other avenues, which we deem social class functional roles, athletics, entertainment, hustling, etc., which are more likely to lead them to economic gain, status, and upward social mobility in the larger societies' capitalist social structure of racial-class inequality over the church and edu-

cation avenues of their white and black bourgeois counterparts of the suburbs.

So even if there were equitable funding of schools, as proposed by opportunity gap theorists, in both the US and American contexts, the academic
gap, we are hypothesizing, would still be present among black males because
of the overwhelming social class functional roles of black males as athletes,
entertainers, hustlers, etc., in the two societies. For black males in the two
societies school and their presence in it is overwhelmingly skewed towards
areas where they are more likely to achieve economic gain, status, and upward mobility, i.e., sports, entertainment, etc. They are more familiar with
the presence and representation of black males as Michael Jordans, Tupacs,
than they are as Cornel West, Michael Eric Dyson, etc. Conversely, the
opportunities available to black woman are more so associated with education as opposed to athletics, the entertainment industry, and the streets.
Hence the reason why black females achieve academically over their black
male counterparts in spite of the so-called opportunity gap highlighted by
Carter and other opportunity gap theorists. Black males simply have more
opportunities to achieve economic gain, status, and upward mobility in the
two societies outside education than their female counterparts. Albeit in the
US many of the opportunities, playing sports especially, are associated with
schools.

Be that as it may, it is our position here that Steele's stereotype threat
theory in emphasizing why black males disidentify with school as a status
marker because of the stereotypical threat it poses to their self-esteem as
opposed to black females where it does not have that stereotypical threat,
overlooks what, ideological apparatuses and their functions, prison and street
life, athletes, entertainers, and hip-hopsters, they (black males) are interpellated by and identify with as their status marker in the society, and the impact
that that identification with such apparatuses and social roles have with their
academic underachievement and or disidentification with school. In other
words, Steele's argument is problematic for three reasons. First, unlike Ogbu
who places other blacks as the cultural reference group by which black
adolescents constitute their identity, which leads to their subsequent underachievement, Steele posits whites and their negative stereotypes of black
intelligence and black internalization of these stereotypes as the locus of
causality for their academic underachievement. In both cases individual responses and scores on standardized tests are attributed to black internalization of cultural group norms, white stereotype norms for Steele and black
adolescent norms for Ogbu. As mentioned in our critique of Ogbu, the reference group should not simply be whites or blacks. Instead, the relational
roles of blacks, and their interpellation by and identification with the ideological apparatuses of these economic social roles within the capitalist social
structure of racial-class inequality of the society should be the reference

point, over white stereotypes and an oppositional culture, or hermeneutical framework for framing and understanding both the black/white and the black male/female academic achievement.

Second, Steele's position, as with Ogbu's, is an *ex post facto* argument regarding the academic achievement gap. That is, it explains the effects of perpetual black academic achievement and why blacks are not putting in the effort to catch-up to their white counterparts, but it does not explain what is the initial locus of causality for that initial effect, i.e., a mismatch of linguistic structure (Mocombe, 2005, 2008, 2010).

Third, the argument is inconsistent. It explains how black women come to identify with school because of their success, and how black men do not identify with school because of their underachievement or lack of success. However, as previously highlighted, to be consistent with its inherent logic, identification with an institution leads to success, the hypothesis should highlight what institutions that black men identify with, their non-dominant cultural capital, that leads to their success, and lack thereof, in the society, and how this identification impacts their academic achievement or underachievement. In other words, in overlooking how their (black males) stereotypical identification with their social class roles as athletes, hip-hopsters, entertainers, and the street-life in the larger society impacts their self-esteem, social status, and lack of academic achievement or identification with school, a partial picture is painted of the framework for conceptualizing and evaluating the black intra-racial gender academic achievement gap.

In this work, in keeping with the socialization argument, we seek to offer a more consistent and sociohistorical comprehensive hermeneutical (structural) framework for conceptualizing and understanding the black male/female intra-racial gender academic achievement gap in the US and UK based on Paul C. Mocombe's (2005, 2010, 2012) "mismatch of linguistic structure and social class function" hypothesis. Mocombe's hypothesis places black social roles within the capitalist social structure of racial-class inequality, mode of production, and its ideological apparatuses as the reference points, over the opportunity gap, white racism or an oppositional culture theory, for conceptualizing and exploring the black academic achievement gap. Suggesting that the black male/female intra-racial gender academic achievement gap is dialectically a result of structural reproduction and differentiation and the social class functions associated with the prison industrial complex, urban street life, athletics, and the entertainment industry where black males overwhelmingly are interpellated and achieve their status, social mobility, and economic gain in the two societies; and the black church/education where black females are interpellated and achieve their status, social mobility, and drive for economic gain via education and professionalization.

THEORY AND METHOD

Essentially, the theoretical framework and argument here is that black male academic underachievement vis-à-vis their white male, white female, and black female counterparts in the US and UK is an epiphenomenon of their socialization and consciousness as determined by their interpellation via the ideological apparatuses of class divisions and their social relations to the mode of production in the societies' capitalist social structure of class inequality. Ogbu and Steele overlook this theoretical framework for more individual analyses vis-à-vis white racism and black opposition to the racism, which overlook the relational and (structural) material framework within which black individual practices and choices take place (Wilson, 1978, 1998). Paul C. Mocombe's (2005, 2008, 2010) structural Marxist "mismatch of linguistic structure and social class function" hypothesis better captures this relational framework for both the US and UK contexts.

Generally speaking, Mocombe posits that black American students academically underachieve vis-à-vis their white and Asian counterparts because of two factors, comprehension, which is grounded in their linguistic structure, African American English Vernacular (AAEV), and the social functions associated with their over-representation in social roles as gangstas, athletes, and entertainers in the American capitalist social structure of class inequality as speakers of AAEV (Mocombe, 2005, 2008, 2010, 2012, 2013; Mocombe and Tomlin, 2010, 2013).

Both factors, "mismatch of linguistic structure and social class function," Mocombe argues, are epiphenomenon of black socialization and interpellation within ideological apparatuses associated with capitalist class divisions and social relations of production. In other words, black American students, contemporarily, have more limited skills in processing information from articles, books, tables, charts, and graphs, and the students who lose the most ground vis-à-vis their white and Asian counterparts are the higher-achieving black children because of language and their social class positions. Early on in their academic careers the poor black social class language game, "black American underclass," who have become the bearers of ideological and linguistic domination for black youth the world over, created by the social relations of capitalism in the US, produces and perpetuates a sociolinguistic status group that reinforces a linguistic structure (Black/African American English Vernacular—BEV or AAEV), which linguistically and functionally renders its young social actors impotent in classrooms where the structure of Standard English is taught. Thus early on (K–5th grade) in their academic careers, many black American inner city youth struggle in the classroom and on standardized test because individually they are linguistically and grammatically having a problem with comprehension, i.e., "a mismatch of linguistic structure," grounded in their (Black or African American English Vernacular) speech patterns or linguistic structure (Mocombe, 2005, 2007, 2009, 2011a, 2011b; Mocombe and Tomlin, 2010, 2013).

This Chomskyian mismatch of linguistic structure component of Mocombe's argument is not a reiteration of the 1960s' "linguistic deficit" hypothesis, which suggested that working-class and minority children were linguistically deprived, and their underdeveloped slangs' and patois' did not allow them to critically think in the classroom (Bereiter and Englemann 1966; Whiteman and Deutsch, 1968; Hess, 1970). On the contrary, as William Labov (1972) brilliantly demonstrated in the case of African American youth they are very capable of analytical and critical thinking within their linguistic structure, Black English Vernacular. As such, what Mocombe posits, building on Chomskyian linguistic philosophy, through his mismatch of linguistic structure hypothesis is that the pattern recognition in the neocortex of the brains of many poor African American inner-city youth is structured by and within the systemicity of Black/African-American English Vernacular (BEV/AAEV). As a result, when they initially enter school there is a phonological, morphosyntactical, and semantical mismatch between BEV/AAEV and the Standard English (SE) utilized in schools to teach and test them. Given the segregation and poverty of many young blacks growing up in the inner-cities of America, they acquire the systemicity of Black English in their homes and early on in their academic careers lack the linguistic flexibility to switch between BEV/AAEV and SE when they take standardized tests. As a result, many black youth have a syntactical problem decoding and understanding phrases and sentences on standardized tests written in Standard English (Kamhi, 1996; Johnson, 2005; Mocombe, 2005, 2007, 2010; Mocombe and Tomlin, 2010, 2013).

Later on in their academic careers as these youth become adolescents and acquire the linguistic flexibility to code switch between BEV/AAEV and SE, the test scores closes dramatically and then widens again by the time they get to middle school. This widening of test scores from middle school onward, according to Mocombe, is a result of the fact that black American students are further disadvantaged by the social class functions (a mismatch of function of the language) this status group, black American underclass, reinforces against those of middle class black and white America within the larger society. That is, success or economic gain and upward mobility amongst this "black underclass," who speak BEV/AAEV, is not measured by identification with and status obtained through education as in the case of black and white American bourgeois middle class standards. On the contrary, athletics, music, hustling, and other activities not "associated" with educational attainment serve as the means to success, economic gain, and upward economic mobility in the US's postindustrial society. Thus effort in school in general suffers, and as a result test scores and grades progressively get lower. Grades and test scores are not only low for those who grow-up in poor inner-cities; it appears to have also increased as academic achievement and/ or social-economic status (SES) rises. "In other words, higher academic achievement and higher social class status are not associated with smaller but rather greater differences in academic achievement" (Gordon, 2006, pg. 25).

It is this epiphenomenon, "mismatch of linguistic social class function," or the social bases of class-specific forms of language use (Bernstein, 1972) of the "mismatch of linguistic structure" many scholars (Ogbu, 1974, 1990, 1991; Coleman, 1988; Carter, 2003, 2005) inappropriately label "the burden of acting white" or oppositional culture amongst black American adolescents, who, males in particular, as they get older turn away from education, not because they feel it is for whites or identify more with the non-dominant cultural capital of the black poor or underclass, but due to the fact that they have rationalized other racialized (i.e., sports, music, pimping, selling drugs, etc.) means or social roles, financed by the upper-class of owners and high-level executives, to economic gain for its own sake other than status obtained through education (Carter, 2003, 2005; Mocombe, 2005, 2007, 2011; Mocombe and Tomlin, 2010, 2013). In America's postindustrial economy, many black American youth (black boys in particular) look to athletes, entertainers, players, gangsters, in and from prison, etc., many of whom are from the black urban underclass, as role models over professionals in fields that require an education. Historically, Mocombe argues, this is a result of racial segregation and black interpellations and relations, within ideological apparatuses, "enframing" the mode of production in America. Moreover, in the age of globalization black communities in other post-industrial economies, like the United Kingdom, for example, are also heavily influenced by the social class functions of the class structure of black America (Mocombe and Tomlin, 2013).

Mocombe and Carol Tomlin (2013) demonstrate this latter phenomenon by extrapolating Mocombe's hypothesis to black British Caribbean youth in the United Kingdom. Mocombe and Tomlin argue because of 1) globalization, 2) the influence of black American religiosity and hip-hop culture via the media industrial complex, and 3) the similar structural experiences of British Caribbean blacks in the inner-cities of the United Kingdom, Mocombe's "mismatch of linguistic structure and social class function" hypothesis also holds true for the academic achievement gap between blacks and whites in the United Kingdom. Black British Caribbean youth, males in particular, overwhelmingly academically underachieve vis-à-vis all other groups in the United Kingdom because of the initial mismatch between Standard British English and Black British Talk, and the social class functional roles associated with the latter among inner-city black British Caribbean youth of British inner-city communities. In this work, we extrapolate the thesis as a hermeneutical framework for conceptualizing and exploring the black intra-racial gender academic achievement gap between black males and females in both the United Kingdom and United States.

DISCUSSION

For Mocombe the locus of causality for the black/white academic achievement gap is grounded in the constitution of black identity and consciousness within class divisions and capitalist relations of production via their interpellation by ideological apparatuses such as education, the black church, media, the streets, athletics, and prisons. As such, Mocombe's thesis is a structural Marxist interpretation of the constitution of black identity and consciousness in that it emphasizes how, in keeping with the structural Marxism of Althusser, the ideological apparatuses of contemporary bourgeois societies interpellates, subjectify, and subsequently subjugate blacks. Blacks, in turn, make choices in the societies based on their interpellations, subjectifications, and subjugations. According to Mocombe (2005, 2009, 2013), ever since their arrival in America two dominant social class language games/groups, a black underclass and a black bourgeois class, created by different ideological apparatuses of the racial-class structural reproduction and differentiation of capitalist processes and practices, have dominated black America. In agricultural slavery beginning in the early eighteenth century, black America was constituted as a racial caste in class dominated by the social class language game of the black bourgeoisie (E. Franklin Frazier's term), the best of the house servants, artisans, and free blacks from the North under the leadership of black Protestant male preachers, which discriminated against the practical consciousness and linguistic system (social class language games) of field slaves and newly arrived Africans, working in agricultural production, who constituted the black underclass. As such, Black English Vernacular emerged among the field slaves whose way of life was juxtaposed against house slaves who identified and patterned their ways of dress, speech, and religiosity after their-white slavemasters in the "big house" (Frazier, 1936).

Deagriculturalization and the industrialization of the northern states coupled with black American migration to the north from the mid-1800s to about the mid-1950s, gave rise to the continual racial-class separation between this urban, educated, and professional class of blacks and former house slaves whose practical consciousness and linguistic system mirrored that of middle class whites, and a Black English speaking black underclass of former agricultural workers seeking, like their black bourgeois counterparts, to be bourgeois, i.e., economic gain, status, and upward economic mobility, through education and industrial work in Northern cities. However, racial discrimination coupled with suburbanization, the rise of the prison industrial complex, and the deindustrialization, or outsourcing of industrial work to Third World countries, of northern cities left the majority of blacks as part of the poor black underclass with limited occupational and educational opportunities, looking to the streets, hustling, athletics, and entertaining as viable means to economic gain, upward mobility, and status (Wilson, 1978; 1998). Consequently, prisons, the street life, entertainment industries became the dominant ideological apparatuses for interpellating and socializing a group of blacks, the black underclass, in the American (industrial) capitalist social structure over the church and education. As such, contemporarily, America's transition from an industrial base to a postindustrial, financialized service, economy beginning in the 1970s positioned black American underclass ideology and language, hip-hop culture, as constituted via ideological apparatuses such as prisons, the streets, etc., as a viable means for black American youth to achieve economic gain, status, and upward economic mobility in the society over education. That is, finance capital in the US beginning in the 1970s began investing in entertainment and other service industries where the segregated inner-city street, prison, language, entertainment, and athletic culture of black America became both a commodity and the means to economic gain for the black poor in America's postindustrial economy, which subsequently outsourced its industrial work to semi-periphery nations thereby blighting the inner-city communities.

Blacks, many of whom migrated to the northern cities from the agricultural south looking for industrial work in the north, became concentrated and segregated in blighted communities where work began to disappear, schools were under funded, and poverty and crime increased due to deindustrialization and suburbanization of northern cities (Wilson, 1993, 1987, 1978). The black migrants, which migrated North with their BEV/AAEV from the agricultural South following the Civil War and later, became segregated sociolinguistic underclass communities, ghettoes, of unemployed laborers looking to illegal, athletic, and entertainment activities (running numbers, pimping, prostitution, drug dealing, robbing, participating in sports, music, etc.) for economic success, status, and upward mobility. Educated in the poorly funded schools of the urban ghettoes, given the process of deindustrialization and the flight of capital to the suburbs and overseas, with no work prospects, many black Americans became part of a permanent *social class language game*, AAEV speaking and poorly educated underclass looking to other activities for economic gain, status, and upward economic mobility. Those who were educated became a part of the Standard-English-speaking black middle class of professionals, i.e., teachers, doctors, lawyers, etc. (the black bourgeoisie), living in the suburbs, while the uneducated or poorly educated constituted the black underclass of the urban ghettoes. Beginning in the late 1980s, finance capital, in order to avoid the oppositional culture to poverty, racism, and classism found among the black underclass, began commodifying and distributing (via the media industrial complex) the underclass black culture for entertainment in the emerging postindustrial service economy of the US over the ideology and language of the black bourgeoisie. Be that as it may, efforts to succeed academically among black Americans, males in particular, which constituted the ideology and language of the black bourgeoisie, paled in comparison to their efforts to succeed as speakers of Black English, athletes, "gangstas," "playas," and entertainers, which became the ideology and language of the black underclass urban youth living in the inner-cities of America. Authentic black American identity became synonymous with black American underclass athletic, entertainment, and hip-hop ideology and language as financed by the upper-class of owners and high-level executives of the entertainment industry over the social class language game of the black middle class.

Hence, contemporarily, in America's postindustrial service economy where multiculturalism, language, and communication skills, pedagogically taught through process approaches to learning, multicultural education, and cooperative group works in school, are keys to succeeding in the postindustrial service labor market, blacks, paradoxically, have an advantage and disadvantage. On the one hand, their bodies and linguistic structure growing up in inner-cities are influenced by the black American underclass who in conjunction with the upper-class of owners and high-level executives have positioned the streets, athletics, and the entertainment industries as the social functions best served by their bodies and linguistic structure in the service economy of the US, which subsequently leads to economic gain, status, and upward social mobility for young urban blacks in the society. This is advantageous because it becomes an authentic black identity by which black American youth can participate in the fabric of the postindustrial social structure. On the other hand, their linguistic structure inhibits them from succeeding academically given the mismatch between their linguistic structure and the function it serves in the postindustrial labor market of the US, and that of Standard English and the function of school as a medium to economic gain, status, and upward social mobility for blacks in the society.

School for many black Americans, especially black boys, in other words, is simply a place for honing their athletic and entertainment skills and hip-hop culture, which they can subsequently profit from in the American postindustrial service economy as their cultural contribution to the American multicultural melting pot. Many black American youth of the inner-cities enter school speaking Black or African American English Vernacular. Their linguistic structure in schooling in postindustrial education, which values the exchange of cultural facts as commodities for the postindustrial economy, is celebrated along with their music and athletics under the umbrella of multicultural education. Therefore, no, or very few, remedial courses are offered to teach them Standard English, which initially leads to poor test scores on standardized tests because the phonology, morphology, and syntax, or the way its expressions are put together to form sentences, of BEV/AAEV juxtaposed against that of Standard English (SE) linguistically prevents many black Americans from the inner-cities early on in their academic careers from grasping the meaning or semantics of phrases and contents of standardized tests, which are written in Standard English. As blacks matriculate through the school system, with their emphasis of succeeding in music and athletics, those who acquire the systemicity of Standard English and succeed become part of the black professional class celebrating the underclass culture, from whence they came, of those who do not make it and therefore dropout of school constituting the black underclass of poorly educated and unemployed social actors looking to the entertainment industry (which celebrates their conditions as a commodity for the labor market) and the streets as their only viable means to economic gain, status, and upward social mobility in blighted inner-city communities.

Hence American blacks, as interpellated (workers) and embourgeoised agents of the American postindustrial capitalist social structure of inequality, represent the most modern (i.e. socialized) people of color, in terms of their "practical consciousness," in the process of homogenizing social actors as agents of the protestant ethic or disciplined workers, producers, and consumers working for owners of production in order to obtain economic gain, status, and upward mobility in the larger American society (Frazier, 1957; Wilson, 1978; Glazer and Moynihan, 1963; Mocombe, 2009). They constitute the American social space in terms of their relation to the means of production in post-industrial capitalist America and its ideological apparatuses, which interpellates and differentiates black America for the most part into two status groups or social class language games, a dwindling middle and upper class (living in suburbia) that numbers about 25 percent of their population (13 percent) and obtain their status as preachers, doctors, athletes, entertainers, lawyers, teachers, and other high-end professional service occupations; and a growing segregated "black underclass" of unemployed and under-employed wage-earners, gangsters, rappers, and athletes occupying poor inner-city communities and schools focused solely on technical skills, multicultural education, athletics, and test-taking for social promotion given the relocation (outsourcing) of industrial and manufacturing jobs to poor periphery and semi-periphery countries and the introduction of low-end post-industrial service jobs and a growing informal economy in American urban-cities. Consequently, the poor performance of black American students, vis-à-vis whites, in education as an ideological apparatus for this post-industrial capitalist sociolinguistic worldview leaves them disproportionately in this growing underclass of laborers, rappers, gangsters, athletes, and entertainers at the bottom of the American postindustrial class social structure of inequality unable to either transform their world as they encounter it, or truly exercise their embourgeoisement given their lack of, what sociologist Pierre Bourdieu (1973, 1984) refers to as, capital (cultural, social, economic, and political).

Ironically, contrary to John Ogbu's (1986) burden of acting white hypothesis, it is due to their indigent (pathological-pathogenic) structural position within the American capitalist social structure of inequality, as opposed to a differing or oppositional cultural ethos from that of the latter, as to the reason why black American school children underachieve vis-à-vis their white counterparts. That is, the majority of black American school students underachieve in school in general and on standardized test in particular, vis-à-vis their white counterparts, not because they possess or are taught (by their peers) at an early age distinct normative cultural values from that of the dominant group of owners and high-level executives in the social structure that transfer into cultural and political conflict in the classroom as an ideological apparatus for these capitalists. To the contrary, black American students underachieve in school because in acquiring the "verbal behavior" of the dominant powers of the social structure in segregated "poor" gentrified inner-city communities which lack good legal jobs and affordable resources that have been outsourced by capital overseas (outsourcing), the majority, who happen to be less educated in the "Standard English" of the society, have reinforced a linguistic (Black English Vernacular) community or status group of rappers, athletes, and entertainers, the black underclass, as the bearers of ideological and linguistic domination for black America, which have been commodified by finance capital to accumulate surplus-value in their postindustrial economy (Mocombe, 2005, 2006, 2011).

It is this "mismatch of linguistic social class function," role conflict, the ideals of middle class black and white bourgeois America against the perceived "pathologies" (functions) of the black underclass as a sociolinguistic status group in the American postindustrial class social structure of inequality, Ogbu and other post-segregationist black middle-class scholars inappropriately label, "acting-white," "culture of poverty," or oppositional culture. Blacks, boys in particular, are neither concealing their academic prowess and abilities when they focus, and defer their efforts, on athletics, music, entertainment, the streets, etc. for fear of acting white as Ogbu suggests, nor do they internalize residual white stereotypes of a remote past. Instead, Mocombe posits they are focusing on racially coded socioeconomic actions or roles commodified in the larger American postindustrial capitalist social structure of inequality that are more likely to lead to economic gain, status, prestige, and upward mobility in the society as defined for, and by, the black underclass financed by finance capital.

The black underclass youth in America's ghettoes has slowly become, since the 1980s, with the financialization of hip-hop culture by record labels such as Sony and others, athletics, and the entertainment industry, the bearers of ideological and linguistic domination for the black youth community in America. Their language and worldview as interpellated by and constituted through the street and prison life, hip-hop culture, athletics, and the entertainment industry financed by finance capital, has become the means by which many black youth (and youth throughout the world) attempt to recursively

reorganize and reproduce their material resource framework against the purposive-rationality of black bourgeois or middle class America interpellated
by and constituted through the church, schools, and professional work that
requires an education. The upper-class of owners and high-level executives
of the American dominated capitalist world-system have capitalized on this
through the commodification of black underclass bodies, culture, and linguistic structure. This is further supported by an American media and popular
culture that glorifies athletes, entertainers, and the "Bling bling," wealth,
diamonds, cars, jewelry, and money of the culture. Hence the aim of many
young black people, black males in particular, in the society is no longer to
seek status, economic gain, and upward mobility through a Protestant Ethic
that stresses hard work, diligence, differed gratification, and education; on
the contrary, a Protestant Ethic that stresses hard work in sports, music,
instant gratification, illegal activities (drug dealing), and skimming are the
dominant means portrayed for their efforts through the entertainment and
athletic industries financed by post-industrial capital. Schools throughout
urban American inner cities are no longer seen as means to a professional
end in order to obtain economic gain, status, and upward mobility, but obstacles to that end because it delays gratification and is not correlative with the
means, social roles, associated with economic success and upward mobility
in black urban America. More black American youth (especially the black
male) want to become, gangstas, hustlers, football and basketball players,
rappers and entertainers, like many of their role models who were raised in
their underclass environments and obtained economic gain and upward mobility that way, over doctors, lawyers, engineers, etc., the social functions
associated with the status symbol of the black and white middle professional
(educated) class of the civil rights generation. Hence the end and social
action remains the same, economic success, status, and upward economic
mobility, only the means to that end have shifted with the rise, financed by
finance capital, of the black underclass as the bearers of ideological and
linguistic domination in black America. Given the reification and commodification of hip-hop culture and the high visibility of blacks in the media and
their charitable works through basketball and football camps and rap concerts, the aforementioned activities have become viable means/professions to
wealth and status in the society's postindustrial economy, which focuses on
services and entertainment for the world's transnational bourgeois class as
the mode of producing surplus-value.

   This linguistic and ideological domination and the ends of the power
elites (rappers, athletes, gangsters, hustlers, pimps) of the black underclass,
"mismatch of linguistic structure and social function," which brings about
the role conflict Ogbu interprets as the burden of acting white, are juxtaposed
against the Protestant Ethic and spirit of capitalism of the black middle and
upper middle educated professional classes represented in the prosperity dis-

course and discursive practices of black professionals and American preachers in the likes of Michael Eric Dyson, TD Jakes, Juanita Bynum, Creflo Dollar, Eddie Long, etc. who push forth with their educated professional counterparts, via the black American church, education, and professional jobs as viable means to prosperity, status, and upward economic gain, i.e., the agential moments of the Protestant Ethic and the spirit of capitalism. Hence, whereas, for agents of the Protestant Ethic and the spirit of capitalism in the likes of Dyson, Jakes, Dollar, Eddie Long, and Juanita Bynum the means to "Bling bling," or the American Dream, is through education and obtaining a professional job as a sign of God's grace and salvation, Rapping, hustling, sports, etc., for younger black Americans growing up in gentrified inner-cities throughout the US, where industrial work has disappeared, represent the means (not education) to the status position of "Bling bling." So what we are suggesting here is that contemporarily many black youth are not "acting white" when education no longer becomes a priority or the means to economic gain, status, and upward mobility, as they get older and consistently (academically) underachieve vis-à-vis whites; they are attempting to be white and achieve bourgeois economic status (the "Bling bling" of cars, diamonds, gold, helicopters, money, etc.) in the society by being "black," speaking Ebonics, rapping, playing sports, hustling, etc., in a racialized post-industrial capitalist social structure wherein the economic status of "blackness" is (over) determined by the white capitalists class of owners and high-level executives and the black proletariats of the West, the black underclass, whose bodies, linguistic structure, way of life, and image ("athletes, hustlers, hip-hopsters") has been reified, commodified (by white and black capitalists), and distributed throughout the world for entertainment, (black) status, and economic purposes in post-industrial capitalist America. This underclass culture as globally promulgated to urban black youth throughout the black diaspora by finance capital via Black Entertainment Television (BET) and other media outlets is counterbalanced or opposed by the bodies, linguistic structure, and images of black preachers promoting the same ethos, The Protestant Ethic and the spirit of capitalism, via the prosperity gospel, patriarchy, misogyny, etc., of the black American churches, to the black administrative bourgeoisies around the world via biblical conversion or salvation, over the so-called pathologies, promiscuity, misogyny, patriarchy, etc., of the black American underclass, as the medium to and for success in the capitalist world-system. Hence, the social structure of class (not racial or cultural worldview) inequality that characterizes the black American social environment is subsequently the relational framework, which black youth and the black administrative bourgeoisie in America and the diaspora are exposed to and socialized in when they encounter globalizing processes through immigration, the outsourcing of work from America, and the images of the entertainment industry and black church. Throughout America, the continent of

Africa, the Caribbean, and black Europe black American charismatic preachers are promoting a prosperity gospel among the black poor and administrative bourgeoisie, which is usually juxtaposed against the emergence of an underclass culture among the youth in these areas influenced by the hip-hop, gangstas, and athletic culture of the black American underclass (Ntarangwi, 2009; Mocombe and Tomlin, 2013; Tomlin et al, 2014).

The aforementioned processes, what Mocombe et al (2014) calls the African-Americanization of the black diaspora, as Mocombe and Tomlin (2013) highlight, is clearly evidenced among black British Caribbean youth in the United Kingdom whose structural experiences parallel that of black Americans in the United States. As such, like the black Americans in the US, the underachievement of black British Caribbean youths is also tied to this mismatch of linguistic structure and social class function, which is an epiphenomenon of the ideological apparatuses of the capitalist social structure of class inequality.

In the Caribbean, most ex-slaves participated in local affairs only marginally more than East Indians during colonialism. In the French and British Caribbean, for instance, whites controlled the local legislature with a handful of men of color who were ideologically and linguistically interpellated and embourgeoised via the church and schools as middle class administrators of the colonial system. The twentieth and twenty-first centuries witnessed a shift in the power in the Caribbean following the end of the colonial system, however. Black and other people of color increased their influence in government and other institutions under the middle class or European influences (embourgeoisement) of the handful of men of color who once ruled with whites during colonialism. Although, the relationship between blacks and whites changed, the continued separation of the black majority from the white and brown minorities meant the poor, who were mainly blacks, developed their own underclass patterns of behavior and beliefs, ideologies and linguistic structures, which became juxtaposed against the middle class and European identities of those in power. Education in the Caribbean, for the most part continued to be an elite privilege. The poor constituted a poorly educated underclass living either in the overcrowded Caribbean capital cities or small farm towns, looking to immigrate to the homeland of their former colonial masters for work and better economic opportunities. The well-to-do, for the most part, paid for private, parochial education; upon completion, they subsequently sent their children abroad for secondary schooling. In many instances, they returned back to the islands where they assumed administrative and bureaucratic roles in government or the private sector. Hence Caribbean society, as well as its immigration pattern overseas, would become juxtaposed between, or against, the poorly educated underclass speakers of Creole or Caribbean patois and an embourgeoised middle class of non-white administrators who, contemporarily, served the same purpose as the handful of colored persons who administered the islands with whites during the colonial period. Be that as it may, upon immigration to places like the UK, racism in the labor, housing, and educational markets, which paralleled what happened to the black American in the US, segregated the majority of the black Caribbean immigrants seeking to achieve the embourgeoisement of their former colonial masters. What developed then was a caste, color, and class system in places like the UK in which the black immigrants sought the embourgeoisement of their former colonial masters through education in segregated poor black communities where work was beginning to disappear to the suburbs or overseas, while simultaneously reproducing a class system in which those who did not attain the middle class ideology and language of the former colonial masters constituted an underclass of poorly educated, unemployed, and patois speaking blacks looking to hustling, the entertainment industry, and sports as viable means to status and upward economic mobility in the UK's emerging postindustrial economy.

Ostensibly, influenced by the success of the black American underclass, who positioned, with the help of finance capital, their underclass bodies, culture, and linguistic structure as viable means to economic gain, status, and upward mobility in America and the global marketplace, black British youth have sought to do the same. They have positioned black British Talk (BBT) and underclass practices, hustling, participating in sports and the entertainment industry, as means or social class roles to status in Britain and the global marketplaces over and against the church professions and educational orientation of the black British and American middle classes of earlier generations who did not perceive their embourgeoisement as the status markers of whites. This has led, as in the case of the black American, to the academic underachievement of black British Caribbean youth due to two factors, a mismatch of linguistic structure (mismatch between black British Talk and Standard British English) when they initially enter school, and later on due to a mismatch of linguistic social class function as they do not apply themselves to academically achieve because of the disconnect between their linguistic structure (black British Talk) and economic success for blacks in the UK and global marketplaces.

Globally, more blacks, of any nationality, are over-represented in the media as having achieved status and upward economic mobility speaking their patois, hustling, playing sports, and entertaining than achieving academically and speaking the *lingua franca* of the power elites. As a result, blacks, black males in particular, are less likely to identify with or place much effort into education, unlike their female counterparts, as a viable means to economic gain, status, and upward mobility in a global marketplace under US hegemony dominated by images of successful black males as hustlers, athletes, and entertainers, social class roles black females are less likely to achieve status, economic gain, or upward economic mobility in. As such, it is within this class dialectic that the black male/female intra-racial gender academic achievement gap in the US and the UK must be framed and studied.

CONCLUSIONS

In sum, within the deductive logic of Mocombe's "mismatch of linguistic structure and social class function" hypothesis, the black intra-racial gender academic achievement gap is a result of the social class functions associated with the media, urban street life, and prisons of postindustrial America and the United Kingdom where young black males are interpellated, over-represented, and predominantly achieve their status, social mobility, and economic gain, and the black church where black females are interpellated, over-represented, and achieve their status, social mobility, and drive for economic gain via education and technical professionalization. In other words, as many black males of the urban cities in the US and UK sought to achieve economic gain, status, and upward social mobility via athletics, entertainment/media industry, and the street life, which led to high school dropout, criminality, imprisonment, and murder rates in the urban inner-cities of postindustrial America and the United Kingdom beginning in the 1980s. Their efforts to achieve academically were superseded by their efforts to succeed via the streets, the entertainment, and athletic industries of industrial and postindustrial America where their bodies and images became embraced by the larger society and its ideological apparatuses. Conversely, given the limited opportunities afforded to black women by the athletic and entertainment industries and the urban street life, they turned to the black church where they found solace from the murder rates and criminality of the cities. Within the church, they encountered a prosperity gospel under the leadership of black charismatic Protestant preachers and educated professionals in the likes of Michael Eric Dyson, TD Jakes, Creflo Dollar, Eddie Long, Juanita Bynum, etc., promoting the same status, economic gain, and upward economic mobility of black urban America and the United Kingdom via the status associated with the church, education, and technical professionalization against the misogyny of the streets, athletic, and entertainment culture of black urban hip-hop America. As a result, black females, who are grossly over-represented in black churches predominantly under the leadership of black male preachers, were more likely to place emphasis on achieving economic gain, status, and upward economic mobility via the church, as prophetesses, evangelists, etc., education, and technical professionalization over the streets, athletic and entertainment industries where their opportunities were limited by young black males who relegated them to dancers and groupies in hip-hop music videos. As such, black womanhood became defined by black educated and professional females who attended church regularly, on the one hand; and those females represented by their depiction in hip-hop music videos and the street-life, on the other. The former esteemed more than the latter.

It is due to this mismatch of linguistic social class function between ideological apparatuses, the church/Jesus and the streets/athletic/entertainment, within the racial-class dynamic of black America and the United Kingdom that the black intra-racial gender academic achievement gap emerged. Black females given their limited opportunities in the streets, entertainment, and athletic culture of post-industrial America and the United Kingdom were, and are, more likely to place their efforts on achieving status, economic gain, and upward social mobility via the church, where education and technical professionalization are emphasized over the lifestyles of the urban street life in both countries where young black males strive and define their manhood via athletics, entertaining, and hustling. It is within this hermeneutical (structural) framework and its ideological apparatuses, i.e., the black church, streets, etc., that black identity and consciousness are interpellated and emerged, and the black male/female intra-racial gender academic achievement gap must be enframed, conceptualized, and explored.

This work explores the sociohistorical origins and nature of this dialectical mismatch of social class functions between the church and the streets as the loci of causality for hermeneutically contextualizing, conceptualizing, and understanding the black male/female academic achievement gap in America and United Kingdom. Chapter one evaluates John Ogbu's and Claude Steele's socialization theories regarding black academic underachievement. Over the oppositional theory of John Ogbu and the disidentification hypothesis of Claude Steele, chapter two outlines Mocombe's neo-Marxian theoretical framework for understanding the constitution of black American and British identity and consciousness within their interpellation in the ideological apparatuses of the (structural) dialectic of class division and social relations of production in American and British societies, which predominantly interpellates and differentiates black America and British Caribbean blacks into two social class language games, a black educated bourgeoisie and a black underclass, which discriminates against groups and subjective experiences arrived-at through the deferment of meaning in ego-centered communicative discourse. Chapter three applies the aforementioned structural Marxist framework and explores the sociohistorical constitution of black American and British identity and consciousness within the dialectic of the American and British capitalist social structures of racial-class inequality. Chapter four, theoretically and methodologically, deduces Paul C. Mocombe's "mismatch of linguistic structure and social class function" hypothesis as the locus of causality for the black/white academic achievement gap in the United States of America and the United Kingdom from the constitution of black American and British identity and consciousness within the dialectic of the American and British Protestant capitalist social structures of class inequality. Chapter five posits Mocombe's mismatch of linguistic structure and social class function hypothesis as an appropriate hermeneutical framework for exploring and understanding the black intra-racial gender academic achievement gap in black America and the United Kingdom over John Ogbu's and Claude Steele's theses. The chapter concludes the work by offering recommendations for future research in exploring and evaluating the black intra-racial gender academic achievement gap in black America and the United Kingdom. In the end, our recommendation for the eradication of the achievement gap is for the reconstitution of the societies and their ideological apparatuses. In other words, our recommendation is not for black leadership to coerce more black males to attend school and church like their female counterparts over adopting the street, prison, athletic, and entertainment life of the urban cities. On the contrary, the emphasis should be on untangling the ideological apparatuses, i.e., the church, education, prisons, etc., of society from capitalists and the mode of production, and orienting them towards the universe and our relations to it and the earth!

Chapter One

Background and Theorizing about the Black Intra-Racial Gender Academic Achievement Gap in the United States and United Kingdom

As previously highlighted in the introduction of this work, in the United States, the academic achievement reading proficiency rate of black males are twice as low as both white males and black females; the employment rate of black men aged 18 to 24 is 30 percent lower than that belonging to young men of other races or nationality; two-thirds of these black males do not attend college compared with approximately 60 percent of both white males and black females; black men make up 40 percent of all prison inmates, but less than 7 percent of the entire population; and they are less likely to attend any form of religious institutions (Steele, 1997; Haskins, 2006; King, 2006; Hanson et al., 2007; Wilson, 2007; Mocombe and Tomlin, 2013). Conversely, black women constitute over 80 percent of the black church; the unemployment rate of black women is nearly 20 percent less than that of black men while in the past three decades the annual mean income of black women has nearly equaled that of black men; black women enroll in college at the same rate as white males and graduate at twice the rate of black men; black women earn 63 percent and 71 percent respectively the number of graduate and professional degrees awarded to all African- Americans (King, 2006; Parker and Orozco, 2008; Cross, 2009).

Similarly in the United Kingdom, the academic achievement rate of black British males on the General Certificate of Secondary Education (GCSE) are twice as low as both white males and black females; black British men aged 16–24 years of age have the highest rates of unemployment, 48 percent, than any other group; black British women are more likely to be employed, 67 percent of the British Labor Market, and earn twice as much as black men; black British Caribbean men 18–24 are overwhelmingly represented in the British prison system vis-à-vis their general population; lastly, black British women constitute over 80 percent of all black church-goers in black British communities (Peach, 1996; Berthoud, 2009; Mocombe and Tomlin, 2013).

As these statistics demonstrate, black females, in both the US and UK, are more likely to attend church, be academically successful, educated, and employed, than their black male counterparts who overwhelmingly are unemployed, associated with athletics, the urban street life, and the criminal justice system of the two societies. In this work, we posit the protestant capitalist social structure of class inequality and its ideological apparatuses, the black church, education, prisons, and the streets, in black communities in the US and UK as the background for "enframing" and exploring the black/white academic achievement gap in general and this intra-racial gender gap between black boys and girls in particular. In other words, the black male/female intra-racial gender academic achievement gap in the United States and United Kingdom is a relational product of black socialization and consciousness (via their interpellation by ideological apparatuses, i.e., the church, education, prisons, athletics, and the streets) as determined or constituted by class divisions and the relations of black male and female social class roles to the mode of production in the two societies. This structural Marxist position opposes the two dominant socialization theories appropriated by social scientists to explain the black male/female intra-racial gender social and academic achievement gap, mainly, John Ogbu's (1986) burden of acting white or oppositional culture hypothesis and Claude Steele's (1997) stereotype threat theory. By emphasizing black individual responses to either white cultural group stereotypes, or an opposition to white culture, Ogbu's and Steele's positions as adopted by many academics overlook the aforementioned structural or relational effects of ideological apparatuses, class division, and social relations of production as the hermeneutical framework or reference points for determining black identification or disindentification with academic achievement gap (Wilson, 1978, 1998). Both positions instead posit that the black intra-racial gender academic achievement gap is a product of disidentification with school amongst black males as opposed to black females as a result of the threat academic achievement poses to either their cultural identities and or self-esteem. Our position, building on the structural Marxist theory of Paul C. Mocombe, agrees with the aforementioned theories in that there is a disidentification with education among black males. However, our position is that the disidentification is a result of ideological apparatuses and social class functional roles not cultural identity and self-esteem as posited by Steele and Ogbu. That is, the theoretical framework for conceptualizing the constitution of black identity and consciousness in general and the academic achievement gap in particular must be black class divisions, their social relations to the means and mode of production in the Protestant capitalist social structure of inequality of the US and UK, and the dominant ideological apparatuses they are interpellated by. Ogbu's and Steele's positions under analyze this relational framework, and as a result should not be considered a complete framework for conceptualizing and framing either the black/white or the black male/female intra-racial gender academic achievement gap. In our view, the black American and British Caribbean are subjects of experience in the Kantian sense, which are interpellated by different ideological apparatuses of their respective capitalist societies. This interpellation and their subsequent subjectification within the racial-class social structure of capitalist society gives rise to black identity and the black/white and black male/female academic achievement test-score gap. The latter two are epiphenomenon of the former.

BACKGROUND OF THE PROBLEM

The education of black British Caribbean students in the UK remains a significant cause for concern ever since their arrival in significant numbers in the 1950s. The inability or unwillingness of the British school system to help young black people fulfill their academic potential has been extensively discussed for the past 40 years (Coard 1971; Rampton 1981; Swann 1985; Sewell 1997; Gillborn & Gipps 1996; Gillborn & Mirza; Majors 2001; Archer & Francis 2007; Tomlinson 2008). This discussion has taken place under the guise of the proverbial black-white academic achievement gap. Hence just as in the United States, the black-white academic achievement gap has also been a focus of research in the UK (Strand, 2012). Research on educational attainment in the UK configures attainment between the main ethnic groups, whites, Asians (Indians, Pakistanis and Bangladeshis), Chinese, and blacks (Caribbean and African). The achievement levels of these various minority groups have increasingly been the focus of much research and debate (Tomlinson, 1984; 2008; Archer, 2003; Chanda-Gool 2006; Archer & Francis 2007; Abbas 2007).

In the UK, concerns about black children and their performance in school were voiced as early as the 1950s. A 1963 study by Brent LEA (Local Education Authority) found the performance of African Caribbean children was on average lower than whites in reading, arithmetic, and spelling. During this period, black children were often placed in low streams and 'remedial' classes or in 'special' schools (Townsend, 1971). The over-representation of black children in schools for the educationally sub-normal, as they were known then, became a very emotive issue in the early seventies discussed eloquently in Coard's (1971) seminal text *How the West Indian Child is*

Made Educationally Subnormal in the British School System. His work, an expression of the deep anger felt by black parents and the black community concerning the education of their children, also acted as a catalyst for central and local government to recognize the problem. However, the Warnock Report (1978) on Special Educational Needs ignored the issue in their report despite the anxieties of parents and some schools.

Throughout the 1970s there was increasing attention to the lower performance of black Caribbean children. For instance, the Inner London Education Authority's Research Statistics Group reported that the reading scores of black Caribbean children were extremely low compared to indigenous white children. While awareness of underachievement grew throughout the 1970s, there was little evidence that attempts to address this issue were effective and black under attainment continued for the next four decades (Tomlinson, 2008). Later studies on achievement in the 1990s also replicated the findings of previous research. In a review of the research on the performance of black and other minority ethnic groups, Gillborn and Gipps (1996, pg. 29) state that, "The relatively lower exam achievement of Caribbean students especially boys, is a common feature in most of the academic and LEA research publications." A further review of studies by Richardson and Wood on 13 Inner London LEAs demonstrated that black Caribbean students were the lowest performing ethnic groups in terms of achieving five or more A*-C General Certificate of Secondary Education (GCSE) the basis of academic achievement at the secondary level. Whilst the national average in 1998 was 46%, for African Caribbean students it was 22% (cited in Hunte, 2004, pg. 32).

Reports of underachievement among black Caribbean students has been documented in a major extensive study by Gillborn & Mirza (2000) utilizing a range of data from 1998 and 1999 from 118 out of the 120 local education authorities (LEAs), and a variety of sources including the 1998 & 2000 Youth Cohort Study (YCS) (a major national survey) and data based on submissions from the Ethnic Minority Achievement Grant (EMAG). Gillborn & Mirza provide ample data from six LEAS to give a comparative analysis of the performance of black students at the baseline assessments, which are assessments based on students' ability at the beginning of their school career, and GCSEs taken towards the end of their schooling. They draw attention to evidence that in each case the performance of black Caribbean students, declines significantly between the beginning and end of their compulsory schooling. In one large authority African Caribbean students enter school as the highest attaining group but leave school not gaining five GCSE grades. A study on Race on the Agenda (ROTA) indicate a relative decline in the performance of African Caribbean between SATS tests at age 11 and GCSE exams taken at 16 (cited in Gillborn & Mirza, 2000, pg. 17).

Social, Class, and Gender

A major feature of Gillborn & Mirza's (2000) research is their inclusion of social class and gender. The link between social class and academic attainment has been established for some time but identification of varied social classes can be problematic. One categorization that Gillborn & Mirza explain, used by many academic writers is the simple distinction between 'manual' and 'non manual' backgrounds where the former can be used as a marker of working class and the latter middle class. Gillborn & Mirza (2000) found that generally students from non-manual backgrounds have significantly higher attainment as a group than their counterparts of the same ethnic origin from manual households, which confirms the strong relationship between class and educational achievement. However, in the case of black British Caribbean students, the social class difference is not as significant; the trend is actually slightly reversed in one cohort. Black students were less likely to attain five GCSE passes than peers of the same social class in any other ethnic group. There has been a decline in their achievement at the beginning of the research period in 1988 when black students were the most successful of the groups from manual backgrounds. During the research period there were points of relative decline in the performance of black Caribbean and Pakistani/Bangladeshi students from both manual and non-manual backgrounds. The findings of Gillborn & Mirza (2000, p. 20) highlight that "inequalities of attainment are now evident for black students regardless of their class background."

In addition to discussions on the social class dimension of black achievement, research has drawn attention to the differences between boys and girls in general, especially in the 1990s when the Department for Education & Employment (DfEE) (Gillborn & Mirza, 2000, pg. 22) reported a significant gap between the attainment of boys and girls with girls having a 10 point lead with 42.8% of boys and 53.4% of girls attaining five grades. It should be pointed out that boys' underachievement is not a consistent trend across subject areas. There are differences in the achievement patterns between the genders in some curriculum areas, with the gains that girls make at GCSE reversed in A (Advanced) Level attainment. Data from the YCS suggest that while the gender gap is now established with girls from the main minority ethnic groups more likely to achieve five higher grade GCSEs than boys of the same ethnic origin and this is consistent with the recent figures reported for 2010/2011 below. There are inequalities of attainment between ethnic groups irrespective of the gender of students. Relying on data from an YCS, Gillborn and Mirza found that although at GCSEs black girls attained more than black boys, their levels of attainment were below white and Indian girls between the periods 1988 and 1995.

From 2003 robust statistical data became available based on students achieving five or more A*-C GCSE including Maths and English. The data provides an accurate reflection of the national trend in education of achievement between the different main ethnic groups. The overall average level of achievement for 2011 is 58 percent. Figure 1, *Key Stage 4: Proportion of Pupils Achieving 5 or More A-C Grades at GCSE or Equivalent Including English and Mathematics GCSEs by Ethnic Group, 2006/07 and 2010/11*, gives a breakdown of the levels of achievement based on ethnicity between 2006/2007 and 2010/2011.

The proportion of students achieving five or more A*-C grades at GCSE or equivalent including English and Mathematics GCSEs continues to vary between the different main ethnic groups. Students of any white background achieved in line with the national level, with 58.0 per cent achieving 5 or more A*-C grades at GCSE or equivalent including English and Mathematics GCSEs, compared with the national level of 58.2 per cent. This score has remained relatively stable since 2009/10. Students of any black background achieved below the national level with 54.3 percent of black students having a gap of 3.8 per cent. This gap has narrowed by 2.0 percentage points from 2009/10 and 4.8 percentage points compared with 2006/07. Black Caribbean students perform lower, 48.6 per cent, than their Black African counterparts with 57.9 per cent. Interestingly, the performance of Black Africans is higher than students of Pakistani origin. Asian students performed above the national level with 61.8 per cent, a gap of 3.6 percentage points. The gap has widened by 1.2 percentage points between 2006/07 and 2010/11. Chinese students are the highest attaining ethnic group. The attainment gap between Chinese students and the national level is 20.4 percentage points, remaining the same from 2009/10. Whilst the numbers of Chinese students achieving the benchmark has increased between 2006/07 and 2010/11, the rate of improvement is slower than other ethnic groups.

Achievement based on gender for all ethnic groups is also a significant feature which is demonstrated in *Table 1 Achievements at GCSE and Equivalent for Pupils at the End of Key Stage 4 by Ethnicity*. Girls outperform boys in the proportion achieving 5 or more A*-C grades at GCSE or equivalent. There is however some variability in the extent of the attainment gaps between girls and boys. The gender gap for Black Caribbean students is 12.5 percentage points, compared with a 5 national gender gap of 7.3 percentage points. Irish students have the lowest variation in attainment by gender, with a gap of 2.1 percentage points.

Further research on ethnicity and education indicates that students of Nigerian origin perform better than their Caribbean counterparts (Demie 2005; Demie et al 2006). The matter is further complicated by recent research which suggests white working class boys on free school meals (FSM) are the lowest achievers in the UK (Cassen & Kingdon, 2007). (Currently,

UK writers use students' eligibility for free school meals (FSM) as an indicator of social disadvantage). However, as Gillborn (2008) points out white non-FSM students have higher success rates than most of their peers of the same gender from different ethnic groups. The greatest inequalities are between white and black Caribbean students and this is true for both genders. Research by Stand (2012) who draws on the Longitudinal Study of Young People in England (LSYPE) also indicates a white British-Black Caribbean achievement gap at age 14. In spite of these fascinating trends many black Caribbean boys are six times more likely than white boys to be excluded from school (DfES, 2006). The scale of the challenge of black underachievement is evidenced by numerous conferences including the annual Black Child Conference in London organized by the Member of Parliament, Diane Abbott.

These similar patterns of black academic underachievement in the UK are evident in the United States as well. In the United States, for example, just 12% of African-American 4th graders have reached proficient or advanced reading levels, while 61% have yet to reach the basic level. In a national assessment of student reading ability, black children scored 16% below white children. Forty-six percent of black adults, compared with 14% of white adults, scored in the lowest category of the National Adult Literacy survey. The results indicate that blacks have more limited skills in processing information from articles, books, tables, charts, and graphs compared with their white counterparts (Gordon, 2006, p. 32). More perplexing, the students who lose the most ground are black males and the higher-achieving black children. Like in the United Kingdom, "[a]s black students move through elementary and middle school…the test-score gaps that separate them from their better-performing white counterparts grow fastest among the most able students and the most slowly for those who start out with below-average academic skills" (Viadero, 2008, p. 1; Mocombe and Tomlin, 2010, 2013). Albeit, by the end of their elementary and high school careers, regardless of their class positions, the majority of blacks, as in the case of the UK, are significantly underachieving vis-à-vis their white counterparts even those who entered school initially performing high. Lastly, the academic achievement reading proficiency rate of black males are twice as low as both white males and black females.

THEORY

A plethora of theories purport to explain this pattern of black academic underachievement in general and the black intra-racial achievement gap in particular in both societies. These theories range from institutional racism (Rampton 1981; Macpherson 1999) and peer group pressure (Sewell 1997;

32   *Chapter 1*

2000; Ogbu, 1986), to more sophisticated models of the wider inequalities in
society, practiced in schools by teachers who exclude pupils on the basis of
their race, class and gender and the intersection of these components (Wright
et al. 2000; Majors 2001; Archer & Francis 2007). Within the last 20 years,
Claude Steele's disidentification theory and John Ogbu's (1986) burden of
acting white hypothesis has dominated both the US and UK contexts not only
in the scholarly journals, but also public policy initiatives, i.e., multicultural
education, mentoring programs, standardization of curriculum, parent involvement, and after-school programming.

    Traditional environmental theories, building on the cultural-ecological
approach of John Ogbu, posits that black American students, given their
racial marginalization within the socioeconomic social structure of American
capitalist society, either developed an oppositional social "identity-in-differential" that defined "certain activities, events, symbols, and meanings as not
appropriate for them because those behaviors, events, symbols, and meanings are characteristic of white Americans" (Fordham and Ogbu 1986, pg.
181), or that such an "underclass" identity stemmed from a "culture of poverty" that devalued educational attainment (Jencks and Phillips, 1998, pg. 10).
This thesis has come to be known in the social science literature as the
oppositional culture thesis (Gordon, 2006; Tyson et al, 2005; Ainsworth-
Darnell and Downey, 1998, 2002; Cook and Ludwig 1998; Wilson, 1998;
Farkas et al, 2002; Steele, 1997; Ogbu, 1991). Both positions, essentially,
argue that the choice between exercising a black cultural ethos and striving
for academic success diametrically oppose one another. Further goes the
argument, this conflict contributes to underachievement among black adolescent students vis-à-vis their white counterparts who do not encounter this
cultural opposition. Black students intentionally underachieve for fear of
being labeled "acting white" by their black adolescent peers.

    For Fordham and Ogbu the "burden of acting white," among black
Americans is a constant phenomenon throughout the United States, which
among black school children has come to be used as a larger oppositional
peer culture with respect to indicators of academic performance and success
(Fordham and Ogbu, 1986, pg. 181). That is to say, as Tyson et al points out,
"academic achievement is not valued in the community because it is perceived as conforming to standard norms of success among white Americans"
(Tyson et al, 2005, pg. 584). This position is complimented by the broader
conservative hypothesis, the culture-of-poverty position, which posits that
impoverished black Americans, the "black underclass," as a cultural community devalue education, "the protestant work ethic," and the two-parent family in favor of instant gratification and episodic violence, which gives rise to
the larger oppositional peer culture prevalent among adolescent school aged
children (Steele, 1990:95-96; Steele, 1992, pg. 75). Within this understanding, black males academically underachieve vis-à-vis their female counter-

parts because they view academic success as the status marker of white males and females, and disidentify with achieving academically and socially for fear of being labeled white by their black male peers. Instead they are more likely to identify with athletics, hip-hop culture, and the street life where they achieve their status in the larger society. Numerous scholars in the United Kingdom have extrapolated Ogbu's theory to black British Caribbean pupils (Wright, 2013; Mocombe and Tomlin, 2010, 2013). Suggesting that the disidentification with school among black males in particular is a result of their social class roles in British society, and their fear of being labeled acting white by their black male peers in the society (Mocombe and Tomlin, 2010, 2013).

Whereas Ogbu focuses on racial and cultural identification, blacks view academic success as the status marker of whites, as the locus of causality for black disidentification with school, Claude Steele focuses on self-esteem and racial stereotype threats. Similarly to Ogbu's hypothesis, Steele's (1997) stereotype threat theory argues that blacks, black Americans, academically underachieve vis-à-vis their white counterparts for fear of confirming the negative racial stereotypes associated with their intellectual abilities, and the threat that association poses to their self-esteem by not blacks, but whites. Within this understanding, black American males disidentify or disconnect with school for fear of confirming black intellectual inferiority, and the threat that fear poses to their racial-identity and self-esteem as determined by whites. The coping strategy implemented by the group at risk for being stereotyped is to disidentify with the domain that poses the threat. In the case of academic achievement, this domain would be school (Steele, 1997). School identification is the central component of stereotype threat theory (Steele, 1998). As a result of their lack of success in school and fear of confirming the stereotypes associated with their lack of success, black males are more likely to disidentify with school as opposed to black females who tend to be more academically sound and successful.

Steele's work, to date, has only been applied to the US context. Yet the notion of disidentification among black British Caribbean males permeates the scholarly literature, albeit not for the racial reasons highlighted by Steele in the case of African Americans. Ogbu's disidentification model thesis appears to be the more explored hypothesis in the case of black British Caribbean youth. We argue here, however, that Steele's disidentification with school as an ideological apparatus within the British context coupled with the oppositional culture thesis reinterpreted within a structural paradigm outlined in Mocombe's mismatch of linguistic structure and social class function hypothesis offers a more complete and comprehensive framework for framing and understanding the constitution of black practical consciousness, the black-white and black male/female academic achievement gaps in both countries.

CRITIQUE OF OGBU AND STEELE

For the most part, researchers have found very little empirical evidence to support Ogbu's oppositional culture hypothesis as either the locus of causality for the black/white academic achievement gap, or the disidentification with school found among black males (Tyson et al, 2005; Carter, 2003, 2005). Instead some opportunity gap scholars in the likes of Prudence Carter (2003, 2005) and Karolyn Tyson (2013) reinterpret the hypothesis as a real struggle inner-city African American youth face between pursuing the dominant cultural capital of the larger American society at the expense of their non-dominant cultural capital of their inner-city communities, which highlights other activities, athletics, hip-hop culture, speaking Black/African-American English, and the street life as status markers. We agree with Carter and Tyson on this non-dominant cultural capital identification with black identity as a more appropriate interpretation of Ogbu's thesis. That is, unlike Steele, who places white stereotype as the status group and frame of reference for black academic underachievement, we agree with Carter and Tyson that the reference group, given black segregation in both countries, should be blacks as Ogbu suggests. However, unlike Carter and Tyson, we see the struggle from a structural as opposed to a postmodern Bourdieuian cultural capital perspective. That is, the conflict as we interpret the opposition found among inner-city African American and black British Caribbean youth is not between different forms of cultural capital vis-à-vis themselves and their white counterparts. Bourdieuian cultural capital is an account of class structural reproduction and differentiation in capitalist societies, not an account of alternative forms of actions, outside of class structural reproduction and differentiation, of cultural practices arrived-at through the deferment of meaning in ego-centered communicative discourse. In other words, Bourdieu's theory is accounting for the agential moments and initiatives associated with class structural differentiation and reproduction, not for alternative practices or agential moments associated with, or that derive from, Jacques Derrida's notion of *différance*, i.e., agential moments arrived-at through the deferment of meaning in ego-centered communicative discourse. Scholars attempt to utilize Pierre Bourdieu's concepts to account for both social agency and Derrida's notion of *différance*. In doing so, however, they are only accounting for capitalist (class) structural reproduction and differentiation via social class roles and practices, which they mis-conceptualize within the language of culture. For consistency, we stick to the language of social structure to offer an account of the black/white achievement gap in general, and the black male/female gender gap in particular in both the US and UK contexts. As such, the conflict as we interpret the opposition found among inner-city African American and black British Caribbean youth is a relational problem between social class roles fostered (via ideological apparatuses such as education, the black church, prisons, athletics, and the streets) in black America and the United Kingdom by the larger societies' capitalist social structure of racial-class inequality, and not their cultural values, which is no different from white America and the United Kingdom, respectively.

In other words, historically speaking, the capitalist social structure of racial-class inequality in both countries via ideological apparatuses such as the media, education, the black church, prisons, and the streets, interpellated and produced two dominant distinct classes in black communities, i.e., a black middle class and an underclass. Their worldviews, "enframed" and structured by the Protestant Ethic and the spirit of capitalism, is no different from their white counterparts. However, what is distinguishable between some blacks and their white counterparts are their class divisions, social relations to production, and the ideological apparatuses they are interpellated by and socialized in (Wilson, 1978, 1998). The majority of educated black middle class professionals are for the most part preachers, teachers, professors, lawyers, doctors, etc., and their practices, acquired via the black church and education as ideological apparatuses, are more in line with that of their white middle class counterparts over the practices of the latter, black underclass, who are interpellated by ideological apparatuses such as the streets, prisons, and the media industrial complex (Wilson, 1978, 1998; Steele, 1998). The latter's, black underclass, practices, like their middle class counterparts, are not cultural but structural. The black underclass tends to be less educated and poor, and as a result constitute social roles and material practices around their poor material conditions. These social roles and poor material practices, attending church, speaking Ebonics or Black British Talk, hustling and pimping, inmates and gangstas, playing sports, and entertaining on the block, which are responses to structural practices, poor housing, prisons, schools, economic opportunities, despair, and ideological apparatuses, prisons, the streets, social welfare, after-school programs, etc., of the inner cities become cultural over generations and in the logic of Prudence Carter and other oppositional cultural theorists. However, their underlying ontology, the Protestant Ethic and the spirit of capitalism, which "enframes" and constitutes them, is the same as in bourgeois black and white America, which seeks status, upward mobility, economic gain, etc. via the church, education, and professional roles over the street life, rapping, playing sports, the entertainment industry, etc. of the black underclass. In fact, members of the black underclass who become successful via the street life, rapping, playing sports eventually become part of the black bourgeoisie or power elites of the society. Highlighting "God-fearing," the nuclear family centered on Christian values, and education as the basis for their success and keys to their embourgeoisement.

Whereas Carter, Tyson, and many other oppositional cultural theorists view the aforementioned opposition between the street life and hip-hop culture on the one hand, and the church and education, on the other, as a conflict between different cultural capital and habitus in Bourdieuian parlance. We view them structurally. That is, we view Pierre Bourdieu's theory and its usage among scholars as a culturalization of capitalist racial-class structural reproduction and differentiation via ideological apparatuses, i.e., the streets, church, prisons, athletics, the media, etc. As a result, we view the black/white academic achievement gap and the disidentification with school among black males in the US and UK as opposed to their female counterparts to be a product of their identification with the dominant social class roles, athletes, entertainers, and the street life, which do not require education or academic success, they as a racial-class group are over-represented as playing in the societies as opposed to the amount of capital they may or may not possess. This is a subtle difference between our position and the oppositional culture theory position. It is not that many blacks (black boys in particular) disidentify with or choose not to place effort or their intelligences on education as the means to achieving economic gain, status, and upward social mobility. Our position is that they choose, as Ogbu and Carter point out, to identify with other ideological apparatuses and avenues, which we deem social class functional roles, athletics, entertainment, urban street life, etc., which are more likely to lead them to economic gain, status, and upward social mobility in their post-industrial societies.

Be that as it may, it is our position here that Steele's stereotype threat theory in emphasizing why black males disidentify with school as a status marker because of the stereotypical threat it poses to their self-esteem as opposed to black females where it does not have that stereotypical threat, overlooks what they (black males) identify as their status marker, i.e., athletes, entertainers, and hip-hopsters, in the society, and the impact that that identification with such social roles have with their academic underachievement and or disidentification with school. In other words, Steele's argument is problematic for three reasons. First, unlike Ogbu who places other blacks as the cultural reference group by which black adolescents constitute their identity, which leads to their subsequent underachievement, Steele posits whites and their negative stereotypes of blacks and black internalization of these stereotypes as the locus of causality for their academic underachievement. In both cases individual responses and scores on standardized tests are attributed to black internalization of cultural group norms, white stereotype norms for Steele and black adolescent norms for Ogbu. As mentioned in our critique of Ogbu, the reference group should not simply be whites or blacks. Instead, the relational roles of blacks, and their identification with these economic social roles and their ideological apparatuses within the capitalist (post-industrial) social structure of racial-class inequality of the society should be the reference point over white stereotypes and an oppositional culture.

Second, Steele's position, like Ogbu's, is an *ex post facto* argument regarding the academic achievement gap. That is, it explains the effects of perpetual black academic achievement and why blacks are not putting in the effort to catch-up to their white counterparts, but it does not explain what is the initial locus of causality for that initial effect, i.e., a mismatch of linguistic structure and social class function (Mocombe, 2005).

Third, the argument is inconsistent. It explains how black women come to identify with school because of their success, and how black men do not identify with school because of their underachievement or lack of success. However, to be consistent with its inherent logic, identification with an institution leads to success, the hypothesis should highlight what institution or ideological apparatuses that black men identify with that leads to their success, and lack thereof, in the society, and how this identification impacts their academic achievement or underachievement. In other words, in overlooking how their (black males) stereotypical identification with their social class roles as athletes, hip-hopsters, entertainers, and the street-life in the larger society impacts their self-esteem, social status, and lack of academic achievement or identification with school, a partial picture is painted of the framework for conceptualizing and evaluating the black intra-racial gender academic achievement gap. In this work, in keeping with the socialization argument, we seek to offer a more consistent and sociohistorical comprehensive hermeneutical (structural) framework for conceptualizing and understanding the black intra-racial gender academic achievement gap in the US and UK based on Paul C. Mocombe's (2005, 2010, 2012; 2013) structural Marxist "mismatch of linguistic structure and social class function" hypothesis, which places black class divisions and social roles within the ideological apparatuses of capitalist social structure of racial-class inequality as the reference point over white racism or an oppositional culture theory. Suggesting that the black/white academic achievement gap in general and the black male/female intra-racial gender academic achievement gap in particular is dialectically a result of structural reproduction and differentiation and the social class functions associated with the urban street life/prisons/athletics/ entertainment where black males overwhelmingly are interpellated and achieve their status, social mobility, and economic gain in the two societies; and the black church/education where black females are more likely to be interpellated and achieve their status, social mobility, and drive for economic gain via education. Both, the church/Jesus and the streets, as we have conceptualized them, are ideological apparatuses of the Protestant ethic and the spirit of capitalism that interpellates and subjectifies blacks within the two societies.

We essentially synthesize Ogbu's and Steele's positions in order to understand both capitalist social milieus. Suggesting that the black intra-racial gender academic achievement gap is dialectically a result of (racial-class) structural reproduction and differentiation and the social class functions associated with the urban street life, athletics and entertainment industries where black males are interpellated, subjectified, and overwhelmingly (overrepresented) achieve (identify) their status, social mobility, and economic gain in the two societies; and the black church and education where black females are overwhelmingly over-represented, interpellated, subjectified, and achieve (identify) their status, social mobility, and drive for economic gain via education. The underlying theoretical position here is that the black/white academic achievement gap in general and the black female/male gap in particular in the United States (US) and the United Kingdom (UK), must be understood as being an epiphenomenon of black historical socialization within the ideological apparatuses of the racial-class divisions and social relations of production of global capitalism. This is a theoretical position that Claude Steele's social psychological analysis overlooks for an individual and racial process, i.e., disidentification because of white stereotypes, which he extrapolates to the group, i.e., all blacks. We suggest Steele's disidentification hypothesis, disidentification with school among black males, is a later phenomenon (because of their interpellation and subjectification in different ideological apparatuses and the social class roles they play in the societies) following black socialization within the racial-class divisions, social relations of production, and ideological apparatuses of the two societies. Similarly, Ogbu's cultural ecological position emphasizes the racial identification of black males to other black males as the locus of causality for the academic achievement gap, and not their class positions and relations to the mode of production within the different ideological apparatuses of the larger societies where they are interpellated, subjectified, and overrepresented. Ogbu's position, as with Steele's, is also a later phenomenon of identification with racial group belonging within the racial-class inequality produced by the ideological apparatuses (prisons, the streets, athletics and entertainment industries) of the racial-class divisions and social relations of production of the two societies. Essentially, both positions, that is, overlook the determinism of the ideological apparatuses of the racial-class positions and relations to the mode of production, and black identification with both as the driving factor behind their theories, the constitution of black identity, consciousness, the black/white academic achievement gap, and the intra-racial gender academic achievement gap. By synthesizing the two positions via a structural Marxist understanding that emphasizes the interpellation, subjectification, overrepresentation, and roles of blacks within certain ideological apparatuses of capitalist society we mitigate their shortcomings for a more comprehensive sociohistorical and relational account of how it is that black males would come to disidentify with schools in both societies because they are overrepresented, interpellated, and subjectified in different ideological apparatuses and social roles from black females.

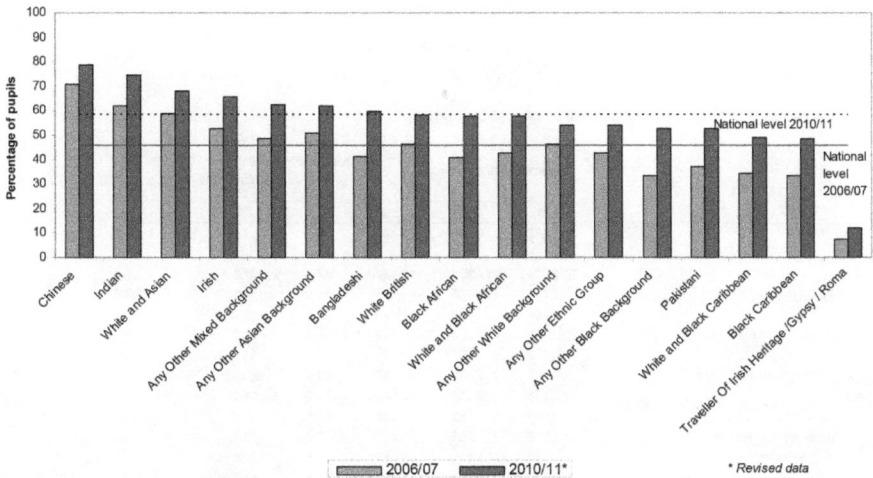

Figure 1. Key Stage 4: Proportion of Pupils Achieving 5 or More A-C Grades at GCSE or Equivalent Including English and Mathematics GCSEs by Ethnic Group, 2006/07 and 2010/11. Source: Department for Education and Skills. Statistical First Release February 2012. http://www.education.gov.uk/rsgateway/DB/SFR/s000977/index.shtml.

Years: 2006/07 to 2010/11 (revised)[2,3]
Coverage: England, maintained schools (including Academies and CTCs)

	All pupils[4]					
	Number of eligible pupils[1]			Percentage achieving 5+ A*-C grades inc. English & mathematics GCSEs		
	Boys	Girls	Total	Boys	Girls	Total
All pupils[5]	**288,887**	**278,045**	**566,932**	**54.6**	**61.9**	**58.2**
White	236,334	227,722	464,056	54.6	61.5	58.0
White British	225,919	217,636	443,555	54.8	61.7	58.2
Irish	984	960	1,944	64.8	67.0	65.9
Traveller of Irish Heritage	67	70	137	19.4	15.7	17.5
Gypsy / Roma	300	295	595	9.7	11.9	10.8
Any other White background	9,064	8,761	17,825	50.7	57.9	54.3
Mixed	9,414	9,361	18,775	54.8	62.2	58.5
White and Black Caribbean	3,161	3,283	6,444	44.5	53.5	49.1
White and Black African	916	895	1,811	53.9	61.5	57.6
White and Asian	1,899	1,860	3,759	63.6	72.6	68.1
Any other mixed background	3,438	3,323	6,761	59.6	65.2	62.3
Asian	22,458	20,749	43,207	57.7	66.2	61.8
Indian	6,702	6,246	12,948	70.5	78.6	74.4
Pakistani	8,683	7,740	16,423	48.9	56.7	52.6
Bangladeshi	3,452	3,498	6,950	56.7	62.7	59.7
Any other Asian background	3,621	3,265	6,886	56.3	68.6	62.2
Black	12,510	12,879	25,389	48.6	59.9	54.3
Black Caribbean	3,984	4,074	8,058	42.3	54.8	48.6
Black African	7,038	7,393	14,431	52.2	63.2	57.9
Any other Black background	1,488	1,412	2,900	48.1	57.4	52.6
Chinese	1,172	1,131	2,303	73.6	83.6	78.5
Any other ethnic group	3,676	3,131	6,807	49.9	58.8	54.0

Source: National Pupil Database

1. Pupils at the end of Key Stage 4 in each academic year.
2. Figures for 2005/06 - 2009/10 are based on final data, 2010/11 figures are based on revised data.
3. From 2009/10 IGCSEs, accredited at time of publication, have been counted as GCSE equivalents and also as English & mathematics GCSEs.
4. Includes pupils for whom free school meal eligibility could not be determined.
5. Includes pupils for whom ethnicity was not obtained, refused or could not be determined.

. = Not applicable.
x = Figures not shown in order to protect confidentiality. See 'Confidentiality' within the SFR text for information on data suppression.

Table 1. Achievements at GCSE and Equivalent for Pupils at the End of Key Stage 4 by Ethnicity. Source: Department for Education and Skills. Statistical First Release. http://www.education.gov.uk/rsgateway/DB/SFR/s000977/index.shtml.

Chapter Two

Theory and Method

Paul C. Mocombe's (2014, 2015) "mismatch of linguistic structure and social class function" hypothesis is a structural Marxist framework for conceptualizing and understanding the constitution of black consciousness, the black/white academic achievement gap, and the intra-racial academic achievement gap. Building on Althusserian Structural Marxism and the duality concept of Structuration theory, Mocombe's hypothesis posits the interpellation, subjectification, and overrepresentation of blacks via ideological apparatuses such as education, the church, the streets, prisons, media, athletics, and the entertainment industries within capitalist social structures of racial-class inequality as the locus of causality for the constitution of black identity and consciousness, the black/white academic achievement gap, and the black intra-racial academic achievement gap in the United States and United Kingdom.

Elaborated in a series of theoretical works and empirical studies, structural Marxist theorists in the likes of Louis Althusser, Raymond Williams, Anthony Giddens, Pierre Bourdieu, Marshall Sahlins, and Jurgen Habermas account for agency and consciousness in social structure or system, "by clamping action and structure together in a notion of 'practice' or 'practises'" (Crothers, 2003, pg. 3). That is, structures are not only external to social actors, enframed in ideological apparatuses as highlighted in the classic structural functional view, but are also internal rules and resources produced and reproduced by actors "unconsciously" (intuitively) in their practices. That is to say, in structurationist or praxis theory, as Marx one-hundred years before suggested, the structure is "not a substantially separable order of reality," but "simply the 'ideal' form in which the totality of 'material' relations . . . are manifested to consciousness. . . "(Sayer, 1987, pg. 84) via ideological apparatuses such as education, the media, church, prisons, etc. From this perspective, accordingly, structure or, sociological speaking, social structure, "may set [(ideological)] conditions to the historical process, but it is dissolved and reformulated in material practice [(through mode of production, language, ideology, and ideological apparatuses)], so that history becomes the realization, in the form of society, of the actual [(embodied rules)] resources people put into play" (Sahlins, 1995 [1981]: 7): consciousness, as a result, refers to "practical consciousness" or the dissolution and reformulation of a social structure's terms (norms, values, resources, prescriptions, and proscriptions) in material practice. Although this duality clamping of action/consciousness and social structure can only account for actions stemming from structural reproduction and differentiation, it cannot account for the actions/consciousnesses originating from Jacques Derrida's notion of *differance*. But that is a moot point, according to Mocombe, for in the case of blacks in America and the diaspora the only blacks that were able to establish an alternative social structure from that of the Protestant Ethic and the spirit of capitalism of the West within which the majority of black consciousness emerged were the Haitians of the provinces under the leadership of houngans, manbos, and bokos.

Be that as it may, from this structural Marxist perspective, the understanding is that race and class distinctions within black communities in the United States (US) and United Kingdom (UK) must be understood as being predominantly constituted within and by the two dominant social class language games, a black bourgeoisie and underclass, created via their interpellation and subjectification by ideological apparatuses such as education, the black church, prisons, the street life, and the media, of the racial class division and social relations of production of global capitalism or the capitalist world-system. The linguistic structures and social class functions that would emerge among blacks as a result of their interpellation and socialization via ideological apparatuses such as education, the black church, the media, prisons, and the streets within the two aforementioned racial-classes of America and Britain would give rise to black consciousness around the aforementioned two classes, the black/white, and black female/male academic underachievement gap. The latter two, Mocombe concludes, are epiphenomenon of the former based on a "mismatch of linguistic structure and social class function," a mismatch between the language that would emerge among the black poor and the social class functions of that language within the labor processes, gangstas, athletes, entertainers, associated with it within the larger society as it differs from the language and social roles of the black bourgeoisie acquired predominantly via ideological apparatuses such as the black church and education (Mocombe and Tomlin, 2013). Albeit once the black poor or underclass acquire economic gain, status, and upward mobility as gangstas, athletes, entertainers, etc. they are interpellated by the larger society as members of the black bourgeoisie. This structural Marxist dialectical perspective stands against Ogbu's cultural-ecological approach, Steele's racial socialization position, and contemporary postmodern and post-structural theories, which focus on local formations, heterogeneity, the diverse, the subjective, the spontaneous, the relative, and the fragmentary as the basis for understanding the constitution of black identities and consciousnesses in the US and UK. The latter positions, we argue in this work are also the product of class division and social relations of production in late postindustrial capitalist development and organization. As a result, they all fail to adequately address the issues regarding the origins and basis for the constitution of black identities and consciousnesses in America and the United Kingdom, the black/white academic achievement gap, and the black/female/male academic achievement gap. They under analyze the relational role of racial-class divisions and social relations of production as produced by ideological apparatuses such as education, the black church, the media, the streets, athletic and entertainment industries, and prisons, and the agential initiatives of blacks. They fail, in other words, because they confuse their attempts to account for agential moments associated with Derrida's notion of *différance* with structural reproduction and differentiation reified as cultural practices or habitus within postindustrial societies. What we argue here, using Paul C. Mocombe's "mismatch of linguistic structure and social class function" hypothesis, is that the logic should remain within capitalist structural reproduction and differentiation as the theoretical framework for understanding the constitution of black identities and consciousnesses in America and the United Kingdom, the black/white academic achievement gap, and the black/female/ male academic achievement gap. The latter two are epiphenomenon of the former.

Hence similarly to black Americans in the United States (US) we are suggesting that the origin of the academic achievement gap among black Caribbean youth in the United Kingdom (UK) is grounded in their historical racial-class relations to the mode of production in the global capitalist world-system, which dates from the slave era, and not to identity politics or the burden of acting white. As Mocombe points out in the case of black America, in agricultural slavery beginning in the early eighteenth century, black America was constituted as a racial caste in class dominated by the social class language game of the black bourgeoisie (E. Franklin Frazier's term), the best of the house servants, artisans, and free blacks from the North, which discriminated against the practical consciousness and linguistic system (social class language games) of field slaves and newly arrived Africans who constituted the black underclass (Mocombe, 2005, 2007). The industrialization of the northern states coupled with black migration to the north from the 1800s to about the mid-1950s, gave rise to the continual racial-class separation between this urban, educated, and professional class of blacks whose practical consciousness and linguistic system mirrored that of middle and upper-middle class whites, and a black underclass of former agricultural workers

seeking, like their black bourgeois counterparts, to be bourgeois, i.e., economic gain, status, and upward economic mobility, through the church, education, and industrial work in Northern cities. However, racial discrimination
coupled with suburbanization and the deindustrialization, or outsourcing of
industrial work to Third World countries, of northern cities left the majority
of blacks as part of the poor black underclass with limited occupational and
educational opportunities. Consequently, contemporarily, America's transition to a postindustrial, financialized service, economy beginning in the
1970s positioned black American underclass ideology and language, hip-hop
culture, as a viable means for black American youth to achieve economic
gain, status, and upward economic mobility in the society over education.
That is, finance capital in the US beginning in the 1970s began investing in
entertainment and other service industries where the segregated inner-city
language, street, prison, entertainment, and athletic culture of black America
became both a commodity and the means to economic gain for the black poor
in America's postindustrial economy, which subsequently outsourced its industrial work to semi-periphery nations thereby blighting the inner-city communities.

Black Americans, many of whom migrated to the Northern cities from the
agricultural South looking for industrial work in the North following the
American Civil War and World War I and II, became concentrated in
blighted communities where work began to disappear, schools were under-
funded, and poverty and crime increased due to deindustrialization and suburbanization of Northern cities. The black migrants, which migrated North
with their BEV/AAEV from the agricultural South, became segregated sociolinguistic underclass communities, ghettoes, of unemployed laborers looking to illegal, athletic, and entertainment activities (running numbers, pimping, prostitution, drug dealing, robbing, participating in sports, music, etc.)
for economic success, status, and upward mobility. Educated in the poorly
funded schools of the urban ghettoes, given the process of deindustrialization
and the flight of capital to the suburbs and overseas, with no work prospects,
many black Americans became part of a permanent, AAEV speaking and
poorly educated underclass looking to other activities for economic gain,
status, and upward economic mobility. Those who were educated became a
part of the Standard-English speaking black middle class of professionals,
i.e., teachers, doctors, lawyers, etc. (the black bourgeoisie), living in the
suburbs, while the uneducated or poorly educated constituted the black
underclass of the urban ghettoes where the streets, prison life, athletics, and
entertainment dominated their being-in-the-world. Beginning in the late
1980s, finance capital, in order to avoid the oppositional culture to poverty,
racism, and classism found among the black American underclass in the
urban ghettoes, began reifying, commodifying, and distributing (via the media industrial complex) the underclass black street, prison, athletics, and

entertainment culture for entertainment in the emerging postindustrial service economy of the US over the church, education, and professional ideology and language of the black bourgeoisie. Be that as it may, efforts to succeed academically among black Americans, which constituted the church, education, and professional ideology and language of the black bourgeoisie, paled in comparison to their efforts to succeed as speakers of Black English, athletes, "gangstas," "playas," and entertainers, which became the ideology and language of the black underclass living in the inner cities of America. Authentic black American identity became synonymous with black underclass hip-hop ideology and language as financed by the upper class of owners and high-level executives of the entertainment industry and reproduced by ideological apparatuses such as the streets, prisons, athletics, entertainment, etc.

Thus, contemporarily, in America's postindustrial service economy where multiculturalism, language, and communication skills, pedagogically taught through process approaches to learning, multicultural education, and cooperative group works in school, are keys to succeeding in the postindustrial labor market, blacks, paradoxically, have an advantage and disadvantage. On the one hand, their linguistic structure growing up in inner cities is influenced by the black underclass who in conjunction with the upper class of owners and high-level executives have positioned the streets, athletics, and the entertainment industries as the social functions best served by their (BEV) linguistic structure in the service economy of the US, which subsequently leads to economic gain, status, and upward social mobility for blacks in the society. This is advantageous for the black underclass because the black underclass identity, the language and social function it promotes, becomes an authentic black identity by which black American youth can define themselves and participate in the athletic and entertainment industry of the postindustrial social structure. On the other hand, their linguistic structure inhibits them from succeeding academically given the mismatch between their linguistic structure and the function it serves in the postindustrial labor market of the US, and that of Standard English and the function of school as a medium to economic gain, status, and upward social mobility for blacks in the society.

School for many blacks, in other words, is simply a place for honing their athletic and entertainment skills and hip-hop culture, which they can subsequently profit from in the American postindustrial economy. Many blacks in America enter school speaking Black or African American English Vernacular. Their linguistic structure in schooling in postindustrial education, which values the exchange of cultural facts as commodities for the postindustrial economy, is celebrated along with their street life, music, and athletics under the umbrella of multicultural education. Therefore, no, or very few, remedial courses are offered to teach them Standard English, which initially leads to poor test scores on standardized tests because the phonology, morphology, semantics, and syntax, or the way its expressions are put together to form sentences, of BEV/AAEV juxtaposed against that of Standard English (SE) prevents many black Americans early on in their academic careers from decoding and grasping the meaning or semantics of phrases and contents of standardized tests, which are written in Standard English. As blacks matriculate through the school system, with their emphasis of succeeding in music and athletics, those who make it academically, athletically, and through the entertainment industry become part of the black professional class celebrating the underclass culture, from whence they came. An underclass constituted of those who do not make it and therefore drop out of school—poorly educated and unemployed social actors looking to the athletic and entertainment industry (which celebrates their conditions as a commodity for the labor market) and the streets as their only viable means to economic gain, status, and upward social mobility in blighted inner-city communities.

Globally this action plays out in the UK, for example, via globalizing forces and the media industrial complex under American hegemony. Given the rise of globalization under American hegemony and the rise of America's postindustrial economy, which focuses on entertainment and service industries, black American athletes and entertainers have become the dominant bearers of ideological and linguistic domination for black youth culture around the globe over their professional counterparts. Thus, in postindustrial economies like the UK, black youth attempt to achieve economic status and upward economic mobility in the society by emulating the language and behavioral patterns of black American athletes and entertainers who, paradoxically, have become global stars and pariahs in the global social relations of production. So it is in the historical and structural evolution of the social relations of production of the capitalist world-system under American hegemony that the black/white achievement gap in America and the United Kingdom must be understood. Black American underclass structural life produced via ideological apparatuses such as the streets, prisons, the media, and athletic and entertainment industries has been commodified by the upper class of owners and high-level executives in the US for capital accumulation in their postindustrial economies. In doing so, they have positioned black underclass ideology and language as the basis for social integration in their society and the world, thereby perpetuating the underachievement of blacks, which began in slavery in the Americas. The same processes we are suggesting hold true for black British Caribbean youth in the UK (Mocombe and Tomlin, 2013).

An increasing number of Caribbean people came to Britain to fill the labor gap in the post-World War II period. In 1951 there were some 15,000 Caribbean newcomers. It is important to mention that America had been the traditional destination for Caribbean people but their entry were restricted because of new legislation, most notably the 1952 McCarren-Warren Act.

Therefore, Britain became the natural focus for migration. The early migrants came from islands that had historic links with Britain such as Jamaica, St Kitts, Barbados, and Montserrat. In some cases British organizations such as the London Transport and regional hospital boards launched recruiting drives in the Caribbean (Walvin, 1984). Many Jamaicans, in particular, were recruited through a network of travel agents. In Barbados, the authorities provided loans and assistance for local migrants.

The extent of population movement varied enormously from island to island. In 1960, for example, 9.2 per cent of Jamaican population and 31.5 per cent of Montserratians emigrated to the United Kingdom, but less than 2 per cent of Trinidadians and Tobagans. It is estimated by the Migrant Services Division of the West Indian Federation Office that the total number of Caribbean immigrants entering the United Kingdom in 1961 was 238,000 (Peach 1968, p. 15). Most early immigrants were young men without dependents (Foner, 1979). Later migrants were mainly women and children. Dodgson (1985, p. 64) captures some of the experiences of Caribbean women who migrated to Britain during this time:

> Life was much harder for women than it was for men . . . I used to have to take the two children to the child-minder and go to work in the factory—I had to catch the bus at half-past five . . . I come back and use the coal fire. They rent you a room but you can't do anything . . . sometimes you had to hide the iron. . . . You think it is little hardness we suffer in this country.

The 1960s saw the enactment of progressively more stringent legislation on immigration. By the 1970s, mass immigration had virtually come to a halt, following the 1971 Immigration Act which put severe restriction on family reunification and chain migration. The total Caribbean population in Britain was estimated at 1.5 percent of the population by 1971. Contemporarily, well over a third of the current Black population is British born and over half of those who are immigrants have been in Britain for more than 30 years. The overall numbers of new immigrants now arriving in Britain is smaller than the numbers returning to the Caribbean. Recent estimates of the Caribbean population provided by the Statistical bulletin (2011) suggests that there are over 600,000 Black Caribbean people (approximately 1.3 per cent) in Britain, of the total population of 55 million. For the most part, British Caribbean blacks come in the main from two social class language groups or games (Ludwig Wittgenstein's term), a patois speaking underclass and an administrative embourgeoised middle and upper middle class created by their historical racial-class relations within the global capitalist social structure of class inequality. In Britain, both groups constitute a small but unassimilated significant black minority which is more reminiscent of America than the Caribbean.

Following slavery in the Caribbean, most ex-slaves participated in local affairs only marginally more than East Indians. In the French and British Caribbean, for instance, whites controlled the local legislature with a handful of men of color who were ideologically and linguistically interpellated and embourgeoised as colored middle class administrators of the colonial system. The twentieth and twenty-first centuries witnessed a shift in the power in the Caribbean following slavery and decolonization, however. Black and other people of color increased their influence in government and other institutions under the middle class or European influences (embourgeoisement) of the handful of men of color who once ruled with whites. Although, the relationship between blacks and whites changed, the continued separation of the black majority from the white and brown minorities meant the poor, who were mainly blacks, developed their own underclass patterns of behavior and beliefs, ideologies and linguistic structures, which became juxtaposed against the middle class and European identities, acquired through formal schooling, of those in power following slavery and decolonization.

Education in the Caribbean, for the most part was an elite privilege for the handful of colored men who once ruled with whites. The poor constituted a poorly educated underclass living either in the overcrowded Caribbean capital cities or small farm towns, looking to immigrate to the homeland of their former colonial masters for work and better economic opportunities. The well-to-do, for the most part, paid for private, parochial education; upon completion, they subsequently sent their children abroad for secondary schooling. In many instances, these privilege elites returned back to the islands where they assumed administrative and bureaucratic roles in government or the private sector. Hence Caribbean society, as well as its immigration pattern overseas, would become juxtaposed between, or against, the poorly educated underclass speakers of Creole or Caribbean patois and an embourgeoised middle class of non-white administrators who, contemporarily, served the same purpose as the handful of colored persons who administered the islands with whites during the colonial period.

Be that as it may, upon immigration to places like the UK beginning in the 1940s, racism in the labor, housing, and educational markets, which paralleled what happened to the black American in the US, segregated the majority of the black Caribbean immigrants seeking to achieve the embourgeoisement of their former colonial masters. What developed then was a caste, color, and class system in places like the UK in which the black immigrants sought the embourgeoisement of their former colonial masters through education in segregated poor black Caribbean communities where work was beginning to disappear to the suburbs or overseas, suburbanization and deindustrialization respectively, while simultaneously reproducing a class system in which those who did not attain the middle class ideology and language of the former colonial masters constituted an underclass of poorly educated, unemployed, and patois speaking blacks looking to hustling in the streets, the entertainment industry, and sports as viable means to status and upward economic mobility in the UK's emerging postindustrial economy.

Subsequently, influenced, via the globalization of the American media, by the success of the black American underclass, who positioned, with the help of corporate finance capital, their underclass culture as viable means to economic gain, status, and upward mobility in America and the global marketplaces' postindustrial economies, black British Caribbean youth beginning around the 1980s sought to do the same as they positioned black British Talk and underclass practices, hustling, participating in sports and the entertainment industry, as means to status in Britain and the global marketplace over and against the church and educational orientation of the black British and American middle classes of earlier generations who did not perceive their embourgeoisement as the status markers of whites. This has led to the academic underachievement, as previously highlighted, of black British youth due to two factors: 1) a mismatch of linguistic structure (phonological, morphosyntactical, and semantical mismatch between black British Talk and Standard British English) when they initially enter school; 2) and later on due to a mismatch of linguistic social class function as they do not apply themselves to academically achieve because of the disconnect between their linguistic structure (black British Talk) and economic success for blacks in the UK and global marketplaces' postindustrial economies where black (British and American) underclass language structures and ideological practices have been commodified by corporate capital for capital accumulation and as a means to economic gain, status, and social mobility for the black poor. Hence, just as in the case of the black American, racial segregation vis-à-vis ideological apparatuses such as the black Caribbean and African Churches, the streets, prisons, athletics, and entertainment industries and the structural processes, deagriculturalization, immigration, industrialization, urbanization, suburbanization, deindustrialization, and postindustrialization, involved in global capitalist relations of production of the last four-hundred years constitute the theoretical framework for understanding the emergence and persistence of the black/white academic achievement gap, which is becoming a global phenomenon as blacks lag behind many racial and ethnic groups academically.

Black socialization, identity, the black/white academic achievement gap, and the black male and female academic achievement gap in the United States and United Kingdom are a product, via ideological apparatuses such as education, the black church, the media, athletic and entertainment industries, prisons, and the streets, of 1) class divisions and black social relations to the mode of production in the US and UK, 2) and the identification of blacks with the two dominant social class language games produced in their fictive communities by the latter processes and ideological apparatuses. So the theoretical assumption here is that the class divisions amongst blacks and their social relations to the mode of production in the US and UK are the basis for the constitution of black (practical) consciousnesses and black academic underachievement as opposed to their internalization of white stereotypes or any opposition they may have to white identity in the two societies. The frame of reference for understanding the black/white academic achievement gap in general and the black male/female intra-racial academic achievement gap in particular, in other words, should be understood within the context of the ideological apparatuses that reproduced the class divisions and social roles blacks play and are socialized in in the two societies as opposed to outdated notions of racial stereotypes or oppositions to a society or social structure they identify with and are seeking to participate in as suggested by Steele and Ogbu, respectively.

Chapter Three

Subject Constitution and Interpellation within Mocombe's Structural Marxism

Within Mocombe's structural Marxist framework highlighted in the previous chapter, subject constitution and interpellation in America and the United Kingdom, contemporarily, is an epiphenomenon of the dialectic of the corporate global capitalist social structure of class inequality and social relations of production, which dates from the 1930s, as reinforced by and through the church, education, streets, prisons, athletics, and the media as ideological apparatuses of such a system. Whereas in previous, mercantile and agricultural, social relations of production in the two capitalist societies the heterosexual and patriarchal family and the church, under the social class language game of rich, white, Protestant, heterosexual, bourgeois, men, were the dominant ideological apparatuses, which attempted to interpellate, control, and direct meaning constitutions and practices, today it is education supported by the media, prisons, police force, athletics, the entertainment industry, etc., which have taken the helm as the dominant ideological apparatuses in place to reproduce the social relations of industrial and postindustrial productions under the social class language game of a multiethnic, cultural, sexual, racial upper-class of owners and high-level executives seeking equality of opportunity, recognition, and distribution with their white counterparts against the underclass language game of their communities and other ways of organizing the world interpellated and subjectified via ideological apparatuses such as athletics, the streets, and prisons.

The liberal bourgeois multiethnic, cultural, sexual, racial, etc., upper class of owners and high-level executives, who sought equality of opportunity, recognition, and distribution with their rich, white, heterosexual, Protestant, male counterparts in their encounter in the mercantile and agricultural mode of reproducing the Protestant ethic and the spirit of capitalism, based in the corporate community of developed countries like the United States and the United Kingdom, represent today's dominant bourgeois capitalist class whose various distributive powers, since the 1960s, lead to a situation where their policies (economic neo-liberal policies) determine the "life chances" of not only local social actors, within the globalizing developed nation, but global ones as well (Bell, 1976; Bourdieu, 1984; Harvey, 1989; Giddens, 1990; Jameson, 1991; Arrighi, 1994; Sklair, 2001; Kellner, 2001; Domhoff, 2002; Mocombe, 2007). As William Domhoff (2002) points out in *Who Rules America*, "The routinized ways of acting in the United States follow from the rules and regulations needed by the corporate community to continue to grow and make profits" (Domhoff, 2002, pg. 181). Globally, this action plays out through US dominated international institutions such as the World Bank (WB), World Trade Organization (WTO), International Monetary Fund (IMF) etc., which prescribe fiscal, political, and social policies to countries in search of aid for development that aids the corporate-driven agenda of the developed world (that is, fits them within the structure of their social relations, i.e., the discourse of the Protestant ethic and its discursive practice, the Spirit of Capitalism), rather than the agenda of the developing countries: the establishment of open markets as the basis for development and social relations in developing countries, whose markets when established are unable to compete with that of competitors in the West, and therefore get usurped by the capitalists of the West who take advantage of the labor force—which is cheapened and exploited in order to compete globally with other—cheaper— prospective markets—and other resources of the developing country, who must allow these investors into their country in order to pay back the debts they owe to the aforementioned international institutions, lest they be declared ineligible for aid and development loans if they do not open up (liberalize) and secure their markets.

From this position, the view is that in the emerging post-development corporate global setting (globalization), globalizing capitalist core states, like the US (i.e., the hegemon of the contemporary world-system), no longer rely exclusively on political and military force to extract concessions, or "market" forces for that matter to reproduce the system or the structure of corporate capitalist social relations amongst their citizens and those in periphery nations. Instead, as Louis Althusser points out in his essay "Ideology and Ideological State Apparatuses" (2001 [1971]), as governing elites in control of the state, as the constitutive element or institution for corporate capitalist bourgeois domination, investors pressure other states to use state "ideological apparatuses" such as prisons, the streets, police force, education, and the media to *interpellate* (name) and embourgeois their "workers and other citizens" with the ideological practice or practical consciousness that justify, and make acceptable, their role (agents of the Protestant ethic of the calling) in the investor/worker/producer/consumer relationship that structures the global capitalist social relation of production as defined by corporations over individual capitalists. In other words, through "ideological state apparatuses," such as prisons, the streets, education, and the media, where the language game (multicultural education, cooperative group works, etc.) of the multiethnic, cultural, sexual, racial, etc., upper-class of owners and high-level executives is taught, social actors in modern societies are named (interpellated) and given (embourgeoised with) the practices and "ethics" needed for both their "ontological security" and the reproduction of the structural terms (i.e., norms, values, prescriptions and proscriptions) of the corporate capitalist social relations of production as it has become constituted and institutionalized by the upper-class of owners and high-level executives of corporations.

Thus, "ideological state apparatuses," such as education, the media, prisons, churches, etc., as they relate to the mode of production, in essence, become the force-less means of socialization and integration to the dominant corporate capitalist order of things. So that in the case of education, for example, in countries like the US and the UK, as an ideological state apparatus in their emergent post-industrial global economy and culture, for examples, the pedagogical practices and curricula are those, which are required to reproduce the consumerist (postindustrial services) means for accumulating capital, which dominates the US and UK corporate economies in the contemporary world-system under American Hegemony. Just the same, the pedagogical practices and curricula of semi-periphery and periphery nations parallel their industrial and agricultural economies, respectively (Mocombe, 2007). The same holds true for the corporate media, i.e., print and television (Bell, 1976; Bourdieu, 1984; Harvey, 1989; Giddens, 1990; Jameson, 1991; Arrighi, 1994; Sklair, 2001; Kellner, 2001). Content and practices are displayed and transmitted in order to reproduce the social relations of productions, i.e., service, consumption, multiculturalism, etc. This fact further implies that the transformation of society rests not on the subjective initiatives of *all* social actors, but on the "objective forces" (discourse), i.e., ideals and practices, individual human rights, freedoms, multiculturalism, equality of opportunity, recognition, and distribution, etc., disseminated through education and the media as ideological apparatuses, which US and UK capital and their pawns (upper and middle transnational class of investors) equate with the nature of reality and existence as such. Hence, whereas those in power positions, multiethnic, cultural, sexual, racial, etc., investors in the global economy, actively partake in the reproduction and transformation of society and the world around them, by (re) configuring the discursive practices (i.e., rules and regulations of the "Spirit of Capitalism") of the ideology (the Protestant discourse) within which their self-interest is best attainable. The majority of workers and other citizens (non-investors), at best, become pawns of the ideology, as they are interpellated and taught, through ideological apparatuses such as education, prisons, churches, police force, and the media, the systemicity or practical consciousness required to recursively reorganize and reproduce, for their ontological security, the discursive practices, social class language games, of power. This is a seemingly non-agential position, for from this perspective social actors of nation-states lack the theoretical and practical skills to transform their world as they encounter it; they simply reproduce it (attempting to live as investors) given their indoctrination—"embourgeoisement," in state ideological apparatuses such as education—into the pragmatics of bourgeois living, which exploits and oppresses the many at the expense of the few seeking economic gain, status, and upward social mobility within the class division and relations of production of the contemporary capitalist world-system dominated by other ideological apparatuses such as the streets and prisons put in place to ensure their socialization to the order of things. This Marxian conception of education and the media as ideological apparatuses for constituting and reproducing corporate economic conditions, social identities, and practices coupled with the black church, the streets and prisons in black communities in the US and UK are keys to contextualizing and understanding the contemporary constitution of black identities, the black/white academic achievement gap, and the intraracial gender gap.

KARL MARX AND LUDWIG WITTGENSTEIN

Within the Althusserian (Marxian) conception of the constitution and reproduction of contemporary societies via mode of production, ideology, and ideological apparatuses outlined above, the class identities and practices (re) produced via the streets, prisons, athletics, education, and the media as ideological apparatuses for the economic conditions of global capital under American corporate hegemony, contemporarily, are twofold: the multiethnic, cultural, sexual, racial, etc., upper-class of owners and high-level executives who own and control the means and forces of production via their work in and through corporations; and the multiethnic, cultural, sexual, racial, etc., workers, social actors of nation-states, who are differentiated by social relations of production and own nothing but their labor power and cultural, ethnic, sexual, racial, etc., resources required by corporate capital, and work for them, and are embourgeoised, via education, the media, and other ideological apparatuses, with the wants, desires, and needs of the multiethnic, cultural, sexual, racial, etc., upper-class of owners and high-level executives in order so that they can achieve economic gain, upward mobility, and status in the society. The former group is interpellated predominantly via education and the media, and the latter, via the streets, police force, prisons, athletics, and the entertainment industry.

As such, in keeping with Karl Marx's class duality in the capitalist constitution of society, what is contemporarily reproduced under the auspices of corporate capitalist relations of production since the 1960s is a twofold class structure in which the multiethnic, cultural, sexual, racial, etc., upper-class of owners and high-level executives of corporations are the bearers of ideological and linguistic domination whose ideas, individual freedoms, human rights, multiculturalism, equality of opportunity, recognition, and distribution, etc., and language are reified and reproduced via education, the media, and other institutions or ideological apparatuses, the streets, prisons, churches, athletic and entertainment industries under their control in order to name (interpellate) and teach (embourgeois) the multiracial, multicultural, multisexual, etc., underclass workers or social actors of nation-states the ideas, practices, and language skills required to achieve economic gain, upward mobility, and status in the social relations of production of the Protestant capitalist world-system. This class dualism, reproduced predominantly via ideological apparatuses such as the media and education under the control of corporations that direct the social relations of production, of capitalist society differs from Marx's earlier conception in that whereas Marx was speaking about personal nature of power or owner-entrepreneurs (capitalists) who owned the means of production juxtaposed against the individual non-owner (proletariat) who possessed only their labor power in the marketplace; in the contemporary postindustrial corporate world, the multiethnic, cultural, sexual, racial, etc., upper-class of owners and high-level executives of corporations, which separates owners and managers, become the bearers of ideological and linguistic domination over the individual capitalist, workers, and society by serving as a collective intelligence and power that institutionalizes and directs the ideas, needs, and practices of individuals and their societies in order to be aligned with the ideas, practices, and profit needs of corporations under American hegemony (Bell, 1976; Harvey, 1989; Giddens, 1990; Jameson, 1991; Arrighi, 1994; Sklair, 2001; Kellner, 2001).

This institutionalization and collectivization of the needs of the individual and society to be syncretized with the economic needs of corporations to grow and earn more profit puts the ideas and language, individual human rights and freedoms, multiculturalism, etc., their language game (Ludwig Wittgenstein's term), of the multiethnic, cultural, sexual, racial, etc., upper-class of owners and high-level executives as the basis for constituting social actors and their societies, via institutions or ideological apparatuses, over the *underclass* language games or forms of being-in-the-world of differing gender, class, racial, and ethnic groups. The Marxian suggestion here is that in postindustrial corporate capitalism the multiethnic, cultural, sexual, racial, etc., upper-class of owners and high-level executives attempt to syncretize the identity, desires, needs, and wants of social actors of nation-states within the social relations of production and class differentiating effects of global capitalism and profit goal of corporations. The aim is for homogenization of ideas and practices within the language game of the multiethnic, cultural, sexual, racial, etc., upper-class of owners and high-level executives who economically, corporately, control institutions or ideological apparatuses so as to prevent differentiation of thoughts and practices, or language games, which arise in ego-centered communicative interactions, from their own em-bourgeoised identities, which stand above and against the underclass practices of those same identities produced as a result of class division, the global social relations of production, and the ideological apparatuses, prisons, the streets, social welfare, etc., put in place to redirect those who fail at, stray from, or are unable to reproduce, the agential moments of the social structure.

It is within this attempt at structural homogenization amidst class differentiation within the language game of the multiethnic, cultural, sexual, racial, etc., upper-class of owners and high-level executives that the phenomenon of black identity, the black/white academic achievement gap, and the intra-racial gender gap in the US and UK must be understood. This continual view of education, for example, where contemporarily bourgeois domination takes place, as an ideological state apparatus for capitalist domination diametrically opposes the position of most contemporary critical theorists of education, who argue for and attempt to demonstrate cultural heterogeneity (i.e., cultural heterogeneous groups engaged, through pedagogical practices that allow for dialogue) in struggles over the production, legitimation, and circulation of particular forms of meaning and experience, within education as a reproductive apparatus for economic conditions (Erevelles, 2000).

(POST)INDUSTRIAL PEDAGOGY

In essence, the argument here is that it is only under the auspices of contemporary economic conditions (postindustrial consumerist globality) under US hegemony that "contemporary" critical theorists of education are able to speak of cultural, sexual, racial, etc., heterogeneity within the existing configuration of capitalist labor power relations and schools. In other words, globalism, globalization/world-system, is a condition of present-day US neoliberal capitalist organization. The process is simply the continual "expansion" of capitalist discursive practices (mostly American dominated), which as Immanuel Wallerstein (1974) points out has always been global in character, across time and space following the financialization and deindustrialization of the American economy beginning in the 1970s.

As many globalization theorists of the postmodernist variety have demonstrated (Bell, 1976; Harvey, 1989; Giddens, 1990; Jameson, 1991; Arrighi, 1994; Sklair, 2001; Kellner, 2001), however, this contemporary (1970 to the

present) condition in the US and UK, for examples, is no longer characterized or driven by the industrial means for accumulating capital, which dominated the social relations of production of the last one hundred years, instead,
the present globalization condition in the US and the United Kingdom is
driven by, postindustrialism (consumerism)—the new means for accumulating capital—and in such "developed" societies like the US and the UK, is
characterized not by the industrial organization of labor, which have been
outsourced to semi-periphery nations, but rather by capitalist service occupations (60–70 percent GDP in both nations) catering to the consumerist demands of a dwindling multiethnic, multiracial, multisexual, multigender,
(transnational) middle class.

The rate of economic gain for its own sake or profit has fallen in industrial production due to labor laws and ecological cost in developed countries
like the US and UK, in other words. Hence, the practice now among investors operating out of the US and UK is financial expansion "in which 'over-
accumulated' capital switches from investments in production and trade, to
investments in finance, property titles, and other claims on future income"
(Trichur, 2005, pg. 165).

Globally, the economic bifurcation defining this current conjuncture,
which began in the 1970s, is characterized, on the one hand, by an expansion
or outsourcing of industrial production into developing or periphery and
semi-periphery countries (China, Brazil, Mexico, India, and South Africa),
where industrialization and the rate of labor exploitation has risen given their
lack of labor laws; and, on the other hand, consumerism of cheaply produced
goods and high-end financial service occupations have come to dominate
developed societies (US, Western Europe, Japan, and Australia).

Hence, socially, the major emphasis among governing elites in this US
dominated global economy or social relation of production has been participation or integration of "others" (specifically "hybrids"), racial, sexual, cultural, etc., who were always present within the social structure, into the
existing configuration of power relations in order to accumulate profits by
servicing the diverse financial wants and cultural, sexual, racial, etc. and
luxurious needs of commodified cultural, sexual, racial, etc. groups throughout the globe that constitute a multiethnic, multiracial, multigender, etc.,
transnational capitalist class. This multiethnic, multiracial, multicultural,
multigender, etc. transnational capitalist class lives a "bourgeois" middle and
upper middle class lifestyle at the expense of their underclass ethnic, racial,
sexual, etc., masses working in low-wage agricultural, manufacturing, and
production jobs, or not at all given the transfer of these jobs overseas to
developing countries. Amidst their exploitation as inexpensive labor con-
comitantly, the underclass practices of the ethnic, racial, cultural, gender, etc.
masses as determined by ideological apparatuses such as the streets, prisons,
athletic and entertainment industries, etc., become cultural, sexual, racial,

etc., markets for the entertainment industry of postindustrial economies that is commodified and marketed by the upper class of owners and high-level executives in developed (postindustrial) countries like the US and UK to the multiethnic, multicultural, multiracial, multisexual transnational bourgeois class for entertainment and conspicuous consumption.

Given that most critical theorists of education have denounced the liberal claim, which sees education as a neutral process, the contemporary debates in educational theory, regarding the role of education in this postindustrial age of the US and UK, which emphasizes global participation of a transnational, transgender, transracial, transsexual, etc., middle class of others so as to service their financial comparative advantage and entertainment needs in core nations, have centered on the degree to which education serves as a reproductive apparatus for economic conditions as opposed to a democratically constructed "discursive space that involves asymmetrical relations of power where both dominant and subordinate groups are engaged in struggles over the production, legitimation, and circulation of particular forms of meaning and experience" in core nation-states such as the US and UK (Erevelles, 2000: 30). Peter McLaren (1988) and Henry Giroux (1992), most conspicuously, given the push for educational reform in consumerist globality, which emphasize participatory pedagogical practices such as literacy and language skills, cooperative group work, multicultural, multiracial, multigender, multisexual, education, and other supposedly cultural specific modes of learning in the US and UK, for examples, "have begun to examine the discursive practices by which student subjectivity (as constructed by race, class, gender, and sexuality) is produced, regulated, and even resisted within the social context of schooling in postindustrial times" (Erevelles, 2000, pg. 25). Thus, challenging the claims of Samuel Bowles and Herbert Gintis (1976), for example, who in *Schooling in Capitalist America* argued "that the history of public education in capitalist America was a reflection of the history of the successes, failures, and contradictions of capitalism itself. In other words, they conceptualized schools as 'ideological state apparatuses,' that, rather than attempting to meet the needs of citizens, instead devised administrative, curricular, and pedagogical practices that reproduced subject positions that sustained [the] exploitative class hierarch[y of capitalism]" (Erevelles, 2000, pg. 28).

McLaren and Giroux, on the contrary, argue that Bowles and Gintis, along with other reproduction theorists such as Basil Bernstein, Pierre Bourdieu, and Immanuel Wallerstein are too deterministic. Hence, influenced by the impact of post-structural theory on cultural studies, McLaren and Giroux among others, instead explore how the everyday actions and cultural practices of students that constitute several subcultures within schools serve as cultural sites that exist in opposition to the hegemonic dictates of capitalist education (Erevelles, 2000, pg. 30).

Our argument here in keeping with the structural logic of Gintis, Bowles, Bourdieu, and Wallerstein is that the Freirean dialogical practices, which McLaren and Giroux emphasize as evidential of the democratic struggle, between diverse groups, over the "production, legitimation, and circulation of particular forms of meaning and experience" within the existing hegemony of postindustrial capitalist education, are in fact the result of the social relations of production in postindustrial capitalist societies, and therefore paradoxically serves capitalist education in core nations such as the US and the UK (Mocombe, 2007).

In other words, the consumerist globality of postindustrial capital fosters the participation of the underclass of cultural, racial, sexual, class, etc. sites that exist in opposition to the dictates of capitalist education. These underclass cultural, racial, sexual, etc., sites, that is the meaning and new identities allowed to be constructed and shared within the ideological apparatuses of the capitalist social space in core nations such as the US and UK put in place to redirect those who fail at, stray from, or are unable to reproduce, the agential moments of the social structure, are used to extract surplus value from their consumer representatives. Underclass cultural, racial, sexual, etc. sites and practices under US and UK economic global hegemony become markets, structured (through education) within the dictates of the Protestant ethic and the spirit of capitalism, to be served by their educated predestined (capitalist class) "hybrid" representatives and the transnational multiethnic, multiracial, multisexual, etc., bourgeois capitalist class, which, working for the multiethnic, cultural, sexual, racial, etc., upper class of owners and high-level executives as middle-managers, service their respective "other" community as petit-bourgeois middle class "hybrid" agents of the Protestant ethic who generate surplus-value, for global capital, through the consumption of cheaply produced products coming out of periphery or developing nations, and as cultural, racial, sexual, etc., markets with capital to be serviced by high-finance capital operating out of the US and UK. No longer is the underclass "other" alienated and marginalized by capital; instead they (i.e., those who exercise their "otherness" as hybrids) are embraced and commodified so that the more socialized or hybridized of their agents can (i.e., through hard work, calculating rationality, etc.) obtain economic gain, status, and prestige in the global marketplace, while oppressing the underclass of their communities, as commodified cultural, racial, sexual, etc., markets with comparative advantages the upper class of owners and high-level executives can commodify, cater to, and service.

These hybrids, characterized by their ethnic, racial, sexual, etc., middle class-ness or embourgeoisement, are pawns for capital, an administrative bourgeoisie that increase the rate of profit for capital through conspicuous consumption, and by servicing the desires, wants, and needs of the oppressed masses of their ethnic, racial, sexual, cultural, etc., communities who within the dialectic of the postindustrial mode of production in core nations like the US and UK become workers, consumers, and cultural producers for the multiethnic, cultural, sexual, racial, etc., upper class of owners and high-level executives who commodify and market their underclass cultural, racial, sexual, ethnic, and gender products to the transnational multiethnic, multicultural, multiracial, multigender, etc. bourgeois capitalist class for entertainment and conspicuous consumption. This is why current pedagogical practices, which reflect Paulo Freire's emphasis on dialogue, i.e., multicultural, multiracial, etc., education, cooperative group work, communications, literacy, language skills, etc., lack the potential, contrarily to Freire's inference, for liberation as they are utilized to reproduce the social relations of production under postindustrial global capitalism amongst previously discriminated against "others," the majority of whom remain oppressed given their lack of social and economic capital due to the "expansion" of industrial production (i.e., loss of jobs to developing countries) and the rise of labor exploitation in developing countries.[2]

(POST)INDUSTRIAL PEDAGOGY IN THE US

Hence critical theorists of education such as McLaren and Giroux under analyze the role of subgroups within education as an ideological apparatus for postindustrial US dominated capital. In other words, they fail to explain how the role of sub-cultures, ethnic, racial, cultural, sexual groups, etc., commodities for capital in postindustrial economies, are embourgeoised to serve such a purpose within education as a continuous ideological space for capital in core nations like the US and UK. Had they done so, it would be clear that the social relations of production of the two, industrialism and postindustrialism, most recent conditions of capitalism are diametrical opposites to say the least, and therefore treat and teach subcultures differently (Bell, 1976).

Under industrial capitalism, for example, "the scientific management movement initiated by Frederick Winslow Taylor in the last decades of the nineteenth century was brought into being . . . in an attempt to apply the methods of science to the increasingly complex problems of the control of labor [in order to maximize profits] in rapidly growing capitalist enterprises" (Braverman, 1998, pg. 59). The end result of this movement was the separation of the roles of worker and management. In the case of postindustrialism (globalization), there was a renewed emphasis on cooperation between worker and management. In both cases, interestingly enough, the techniques and functions of the work place were replicated in US classrooms to serve as the means of socialization or enculturation to the labor process, and its subsequent way of life.

This direct correlation, most conspicuously, was between the implementation of pedagogical practices in American classrooms that paralleled the organization of work under each mode of production (Mocombe, 2001, 2007; Mocombe and Tomlin, 2010, 2013). For instance, under the scientific movement of the industrial stage, mental work was separated from manual work, and "a necessary consequence of this separation [was] that the labor process [became] divided between separate sites and separate bodies of workers. In one location, the physical processes of production [were] executed. In another [were] concentrated the design, planning, calculation, and record-keeping. The preconception of the process before it is set in motion, the visualization of each worker's activities before they have actually begun, the definition of each function along with the manner of its performance and the time it will consume, the control and checking of the ongoing process once it is under way, and the assessment of results upon completion of each stage of the process—all of these aspects of production [were] removed from the shop floor to the management office" (Braverman, 1998, pg. 86).

To parallel the concepts of control adopted by management at that time, school curricula in the US stressed marching, drill, orderliness, assigned seats in rows, individualized seatwork, and tracking and leveling; seemingly all were preparation for the coordination and orderliness required in the modern factory. Lining up for class as well as marching in and out of the cloakroom and to the blackboard were activities justified in terms of training for factory assembly lines, while tracking and leveling sorted out future workers and managers (Springs, 1994, pg. 18).

In short, all of the above-mentioned vestiges of the school curriculum/ pedagogy complimented an aspect of the factory under scientific-management, and sought uniformity of practice while discriminating against and marginalizing cultural, racial, ethnic, sexual, etc., groups. This is why, the service-oriented (postindustrialism) restructuring of American capitalist society, beginning in the 1960s, witnessed massive reform initiatives in school pedagogies—a result of postindustrialization of the American economy, outsourcing of work to the Third World, and the diverse, feminist, gay and lesbian, black, etc., movements for equality of opportunity, recognition, and distribution within the class division and social relations of production of the Protestant Ethic and the spirit of capitalism, which led to the reconceptualization of the role of the worker in the labor-process under consumerist globality. Skills that were peculiar to the industrial worker become futile to the service worker in the postindustrial process. That is, whereas, the old work process was founded on passive submission to schedules or routines, individualism, isolationism, and privatism; the postindustrial or globalization stage of the labor process focuses on teamwork. "It celebrates sensitivity to others; it requires such 'soft skills' as being a good listener and being cooperative" (Sennett, 1998, pg. 99).

This reorganization of work has revamped the role of the laborer in the work process, and "throughout the U.S. economy, employers and managers are promoting a new ethos of participation for their workers. In fact, the spread of a paradigm of participation—comprised of extensive discussion about the merits of worker involvement as well as actual transformation of production methods and staffing practices—may indeed be one of the most significant trends sweeping across postindustrial, late twentieth-century workplaces" (Smith, 1998, pg. 460).

To ensure socialization to this new aspect of *Being* in (post)capitalism, this trend of employee involvement is adumbrated in the pedagogical curriculum reform movements of many US school systems, which place a major emphasis on literacy and language skills, "process approaches," "active learning strategies," such as multicultural education, cooperative learning, group work, and many other "soft skills"—good listener, speaker, reader, and writer—which characterize the dialogical and service elements of the new labor-process.

This paradigm of participation, accordingly, is not an attempt on behalf of management to reassociate the conception of work with its execution. In other words, this is neither a reconstruction of Taylorism's principles nor a means of trying to liberate the workers, as a result of the subsequent dialogue brought on by this ethos of participation. Instead, "Sociologists, industrial relations researchers, organizational scientists, and policymakers who have studied this trend agree that leaders and managers of U.S. companies are climbing aboard the bandwagon of worker participation in their urgent attempts to maintain competitiveness under changing economic circumstances. Employers believe that when workers participate in making decisions, when they gain opportunities to apply their tacit knowledge to problem solving, and when they acquire responsibility for designing and directing production processes, they feed into an infrastructure enabling firms to respond to shifting market and product demands [consumer demands] in a rapid and timely way" (Smith, 1998, pg. 460).

This is the fundamental reason why the existing configurations of economic hegemonic power, located in the US and UK, contemporarily, allow for the fashioning and participation of new identities (through pedagogical practices that engender participation, i.e., cooperative group work, field trips, class room presentations, multicultural education, communications, etc.) in the order of things: under industrial capitalism the aim of the upper class of owners and high-level executives was accumulation of capital through the industrial production of cheaply produced goods for the dominating masses and those in militarily controlled overseas markets (hence the rise of surplus-value at the expense of labor exploitation in industrial jobs); under postindustrialism, however, the emphasis is financially servicing and entertaining a larger segment of these markets, not just the initial colonial "hybrid" petit-bourgeois class, who are also interested in obtaining a larger portion of these markets as members of a dwindling (transnational, transgender, transracial, etc.,) middle class interpellated by, and "embourgeoised" with the wants and needs of, capital (hence the fall of the rate of profit) seeking equality of opportunity, recognition, and distribution with them. This transnational multiethnic, multiracial, multicultural, multigender, etc., middle class, which is a result of the restructuring of the organization of labor (service-oriented in the First World or core nations, production in the Third or developing world), which no longer discriminates and marginalize these groups, by the dominant bourgeois class of owners and high-level executives in core countries in order to increase the rate of profit or accumulate more capital beginning in the 1970s, constitute the capitalist social space as pawns or service-workers, who service the desires, wants, and needs of the oppressed of their respective communities—who are either unemployed or work in labor intensive production jobs—while at the same time legitimating the "hybrid" petit-bourgeois multiethnic, cultural, sexual, racial, etc., middle class identities, which the multiethnic, cultural, sexual, racial, etc., oppressed masses, working in low-wage earning occupations or not at all, must aspire to, while producing surplus-value (increasing the rate of profit) for capital through labor, entertainment production, tourism, and consumption.

Thus, in the socialization of "identities-in-differential" within education as an ideological apparatus for the postindustrial capitalist social structure what is (re)produced is ideological sameness amongst diverse "bodies/subjects" vying for control of their commodified oppressed markets as firms, who employ the more integrated or socialized amongst them, embourgeoised "hybrids," learn, by using the knowledge which dialogue between subjective positions foster, how to maximize their profits by catering to the financial, entertainment, and consumptive needs of these "new" consumers represented by "hybrids," i.e., "other" agents of the Protestant ethic and the spirit of capitalism, of their underclass communities.

Thus, the introduction of management-initiated employee involvement programs (EIPs), as well as paralleling pedagogical practices (literacy and language skills, dialogue, cooperative group work, multiculturalism, "soft skills," i.e., good listener, etc.) in schools, have been introduced in postindustrial places like the US and UK, under the auspices and practical consciousness of the "hybrid" class of once discriminated against identities, who have sided with capital, in order to obtain profit through auxiliary service occupations—consumerism, the current means of capital accumulation, currently dominating the globalization process or, as Wallerstein three decades ago framed it, the "world-economy"—controlled by capital, who continues to oppress and marginalize the multiethnic, cultural, sexual, racial, etc., poor it creates in developing countries through the outsourcing of low-wage production and agricultural jobs to keep down the cost of labor and extract surplus-value.

In this sense, education in postindustrial economies like that of the US and UK is no longer a discursive space where student subjectivity, as constructed by race, class, gender, and sexuality is given free reign to develop; on the contrary, their subjectivity, as constructed by race, class, gender, and sexuality is (re)produced and regulated by hybrid bourgeois constructions determined by ideological apparatuses and their relation to the means of production. In other words, the discourse and discursive practices of racial, class, gender, and sexual identities in postindustrial economies like the US and UK are commodified and reified around their historical social relations to the mode of production so that finance capital can cater to and service their consumption needs while simultaneously commodifying their underclass discourse and discursive practices, "mobilization of the spectacle," for consumption by global others who are similarly situated. Hence, inequalities and identities within racial, class, gender, and sexual groups in postindustrial economies are institutionalized around their inequalities and identities and they (their inequalities and identities) become the means by which their respective members must attempt to seek economic gain, status, and prestige in the societies.

That is to say, in contemporary postindustrial capitalist societies racial, class, gender, and sexual groups are commodified and integrated around their relations to the mode of production. Integrating, typically speaking, in the society around two *social class language games*, a multiethnic, cultural, sexual, racial, etc., educated professional class of teachers, lawyers, doctors, etc., who in language and social class practices are indistinguishable from the multiethnic, cultural, sexual, racial, etc., upper class of owners and high-level executives, and a multiethnic, cultural, sexual, racial, etc., urban underclass of unemployed laborers looking to profit from their identities, which are constituted around their linguistic and economic segregation from the multiethnic, cultural, sexual, racial, etc., educated professional class and upper class of owners and high-level executives, in the postindustrial economy. What we are suggesting here is that in postindustrial economies like the US and UK, the identities of racial, class, gender, and sexual groups are commodified by the upper class of owners and high-level executives around their social class identities determined by their historical relations to the mode of production reproduced via ideological apparatuses. That is, they are commodified around their class positions or *habitus* within the capitalist social structure, and come to constitute two social class language games: one determined by their degree of socialization and assimilation, via education, in the dominant linguistic community or language game of the multiethnic, cultural, sexual, racial, etc., upper class of owners and high-level executives; and the other, determined by their poverty and lack of socialization. The latter group, because of its poverty and lack of socialization is segregated in poor social spaces with institutions or ideological apparatuses, pawn shops, liquor stores, check cashing stores, the streets where they hustle, prisons, etc., that cater to and foster their poverty from the former, and constitutes their own rule-governed, self-contained practice of activities associated with achieving success, like their middle class and better educated counterparts, within the capitalist social structure, without, however, abandoning their language game which, although marginalized by their more educated compatriots, is not marginalized by the multiethnic, cultural, sexual, racial, etc., upper class of owners and high-level executives who commodify it for profit in the enter-tainment/service industries of postindustrial economies like that of the US and UK.

As a result, in postindustrial economies both the underclass and middle class identities of racial, class, gender, and sexual groups become viable identity markers for achieving economic gain, status, and upward social mo-bility to the chagrin of middle class hybrid others who do not view the underclass language game of their community as legitimate. Just the same, members of the underclass hybrid community also do not view the middle class hybrid identity of their compatriots as legitimate. However, whereas under industrialism the middle class identity was the bearer of ideological and linguistic domination, in postindustrialism, the billion dollar entertain-ment and service economy financed by the upper class of owners and high-level executives has also privileged the underclass identity of racial, class, gender, and sexual groups as the bearer of ideological and linguistic domina-tion for economic gain. Hence the language game of the middle class hybrid other, with its emphasis on speaking Standard English or the language of the dominant group, education as the viable means to status, and emulating the lifestyles of the multiethnic, cultural, sexual, racial, etc., upper class of own-ers and high-level executives, is no longer the sole basis for success. It has been supplemented and in some regards supplanted by the language game of the underclass identity of racial, class, gender, and sexual groups, which continue to be differentiated by class division and the social relations of production reproduced via ideological apparatuses such as education, the media, church, the streets, prisons, etc.

Black consciousness and communities in the US and UK, as highlighted in the previous chapters, are the by-product of the global (industrial and postindustrial) capitalist social structure of class inequality and differentia-tion reproduced via ideological apparatuses, which attempt to structure the practices of subjective experiences within class differentiation and thereby direct and control the practices of diversity and meaning constitution. So the theoretical assumptions here is that it is within the class division and social relations of production promulgated via ideological apparatuses such as edu-cation, the black church, media, prisons, police force, and the streets that

black American and British identities/practical consciousnesses, the black/
white academic achievement gap, and the intra-racial gender gap must be
understood.

NOTES

1. Our reading of globalization completely breaks away from critical social theorists (Gild-
er 1989, 2000; Kaku, 1997; Kellner), who see globalization as an integral part of the scientific
and technological revolutions of the modern era. I believe it is not necessarily the case that the
scientific and technological revolutions of the modern era should give rise to present global
processes; in fact, the networking of people, ideas, forms of culture, and people across national
boundaries has been an integral aspect of human culture. So much so that I would venture to
call it a natural process. Thus, for me, "modern" globalization is a movement whereby a
dominant culture, i.e., bourgeois capitalist culture of the West (America and Western Europe),
attempts to reproduce its way of life by integrating the world's population into its structures of
signification, i.e., freedom, democracy, increased wealth, and happiness (the Protestant ethic).
All of this is accomplished through a set of social relations directed and controlled by the
market, military power, and supervisory institutions such as the U.N.

2. Essentially, this is also the basis for contemporary struggles over educational testing
reform, i.e., the necessary push to reassess and reconfigure the testing tools within postindustrial societies.

Chapter Four

Black Subject Constitution and Interpellation in the US and UK within Mocombe's Structural Marxism

Black consciousness in the US and UK is a product of ideological apparatuses, class divisions, and the social relations of production in the two capitalist social structures of class inequality. The black/white academic achievement gap is an epiphenomenon of the aforementioned processes. Essentially, the theoretical assumption here is that black male academic underachievement vis-à-vis their white male, white female, and black female counterparts in the US and UK is an epiphenomenon of their interpellation, socialization, and practical consciousness as determined by class divisions and their social relations to the mode of production in the societies' capitalist social structure of class inequality reproduced via ideological apparatuses such as education, the streets, prisons, police force, entertainment industry, media, athletics, etc. Ogbu and Steele overlook this theoretical framework for more individual analyses vis-à-vis white racism and black opposition to the racism, which overlooks the relational framework and other ideological apparatuses, aside from education, within which black identity is constituted and individual practices and choices take place (Wilson, 1978, 1987, 1998). Paul C. Mocombe's structural Marxist understanding of the constitution of black identity in the US and UK highlighted in the previous chapters supplants white stereotypes and black opposition with class divisions, social class roles, and ideological apparatuses as the reference points for the interpellation and constitution of black identity and the black academic underachievement gap vis-à-vis whites and black females.

Black consciousness and identity is a product of their interpellation by and socialization in via ideological apparatuses such as the black church, education, prison, the media, athletic and entertainment industries, and the streets, within the capitalist social structure of class inequality, which differentiates, based on their social relations to the means/mode of production, blacks into two social class language games, a black upper/middle class and an underclass. The black/white academic achievement gap is an epiphenomenon of black interpellation, identification, and socialization within the social class language game of the black underclass as determined by their relations to the mode of production. This is Paul C. Mocombe's "mismatch of linguistic structure and social class function" hypothesis.

In terms of the black/white academic achievement gap, Mocombe's mismatch of linguistic structure and social class function hypothesis posits that black American students academically underachieve vis-à-vis their white and Asian counterparts because of two factors, comprehension, which is grounded in their linguistic structure, African American English Vernacular (AAEV), and the social functions associated with their over-representation in social roles as criminals, athletes, and entertainers in the American capitalist social structure of class inequality as speakers of AAEV (Mocombe, 2005, 2008, 2010, 2012, 2013; Mocombe and Tomlin, 2013). In other words, black American students, contemporarily, have more limited skills in processing information from articles, books, tables, charts, and graphs, and the students who lose the most ground vis-à-vis their white and Asian counterparts are the higher-achieving black children because early on in their academic careers the poor black social class language game, "black American underclass," have become the bearers of ideological and linguistic domination for black youth the world over. Created by the social relations of capitalism in the US, they produce and perpetuate a sociolinguistic status group that reinforces a linguistic structure (Black/African American English Vernacular—BEV or AAEV), which linguistically and functionally renders its young social actors impotent in classrooms where the structure of Standard English is taught. Thus early on (K–5th grade) in their academic careers, many black American inner city youth struggle in the classroom and on standardized test because individually they are linguistically and grammatically having a problem with comprehension, i.e., "a mismatch of linguistic structure," grounded in their (Black or African American English Vernacular) speech patterns or linguistic structure (Mocombe, 2005, 2007, 2009, 2011a, 2011b; Mocombe and Tomlin, 2010, 2013).

This mismatch of linguistic structure component of Mocombe's argument is not a reiteration of the 1960s' "linguistic deficit" hypothesis, which suggested that working-class and minority children were linguistically deprived, and their underdeveloped slangs' and patois' did not allow them to critically think in the classroom (Bereiter and Englemann 1966; Whiteman and Deutsch, 1968; Hess, 1970). On the contrary, as William Labov (1972) brilliantly demonstrated in the case of African American youth they are very capable of analytical and critical thinking within their linguistic structure, Black English Vernacular. What Mocombe posits through his mismatch of linguistic structure hypothesis is that the pattern recognition in the neocortex of the brains of many poor African American inner-city youth is structured by and within the systemicity of Black/African-American English Vernacular (BEV/AAEV). As a result, when they initially enter school there is a phonological, morphosyntactical, and semantical mismatch between BEV/AAEV and the Standard English (SE) utilized in schools to teach and test them. Given the segregation and poverty of many young blacks growing up in the inner-cities of America, they acquire the systemicity of Black English and early on in their academic careers lack the linguistic flexibility to switch between BEV/AAEV and SE when they take standardized tests. As a result, many black youth have a syntactical problem decoding and understanding phrases and sentences on standardized tests written in Standard English (Kamhi, 1996; Johnson, 2005; Mocombe, 2010; Mocombe and Tomlin, 2010, 2013).

Later on in their academic careers as these youth become adolescents and acquire the linguistic flexibility to code switch between BEV/AAEV and SE, the test scores closes dramatically and then widens again by the time they get to middle school (Mocombe, 2010; Mocombe and Tomlin, 2010, 2013). This widening of test scores from middle school onward, according to Mocombe, is a result of the fact that black American students are further disadvantaged by the social class functions (a mismatch of function of the language) this status group, black American underclass, reinforces against those of middle class black and white America. That is, success or economic gain and upward mobility amongst this "black underclass," who speak BEV/AAEV, is not measured by status obtained through the church and education as in the case of black and white American bourgeois middle class standards. On the contrary, athletics, music, and other activities not "associated" with educational attainment serve as the means to success, economic gain, and upward economic mobility in the US's postindustrial society. Thus effort in school in general suffers, and as a result test scores and grades progressively get lower. Grades and test scores are not only low for those who grow-up in poor-inner cities, it appears to have also increased as academic achievement and/ or social-economic status (SES) rises. "In other words, higher academic achievement and higher social class status are not associated with smaller but rather greater differences in academic achievement" (Gordon, 2006, pg. 25).

It is this epiphenomenon, "mismatch of linguistic social class function," or the social bases of class-specific forms of language use (Bernstein, 1972) of the "mismatch of linguistic structure" many scholars (Ogbu, 1974, 1990, 1991; Coleman, 1988; Carter, 2003, 2005) inappropriately label disidentification, "the burden of acting white" or oppositional culture amongst black American adolescents, who, males in particular, as they get older turn away from education, not because they feel it is for whites or identify more with the non-dominant cultural capital of the black poor or underclass, but due to the fact that they have rationalized other racialized (i.e., sports, music, pimping, selling drugs, etc.) means or social roles, financed by the upper-class of owners and high-level executives, to economic gain for its own sake other than status obtained through education (Carter, 2003, 2005; Mocombe, 2005, 2007, 2011; Mocombe and Tomlin, 2010, 2013). In America's postindustrial economy, many black American youth (black boys in particular) look to athletes, entertainers, players, gangsters, etc., many of whom are from the black urban underclass, as role models over professionals in fields that require an education. Historically, Mocombe argues, this is a result of ideological apparatuses, racial segregation, and black relations to the mode of production in America, and in the age of globalization black communities in other post-industrial economies, like the United Kingdom, for example, are also heavily influenced by the social class functions of the class structure of black America.

Mocombe and Carol Tomlin demonstrate this latter phenomenon by extrapolating the hypothesis to black British Caribbean youth in the United Kingdom (Mocombe and Tomlin, 2010, 2013). Mocombe and Tomlin argue because of 1) globalization, 2) the influence of black American hip-hop culture and the black church, and 3) the similar structural experiences of British Caribbean blacks in the inner-cities of the United Kingdom, Mocombe's "mismatch of linguistic structure and social class function" hypothesis also holds true for the academic achievement gap between blacks and whites in the United Kingdom. Black British Caribbean youth, males in particular, overwhelmingly academically underachieve vis-à-vis all other groups in the United Kingdom because of the initial mismatch between Standard British English and Black British Talk, and the social class functional roles associated with the latter among inner-city black British Caribbean youth of British inner-city communities.

According to Mocombe (2005, 2009, 2012), ever since their arrival in America two dominant social class language games/groups, a black underclass and a black bourgeois class, created by the racial-class structural reproduction and differentiation of capitalist processes, practices, and ideological apparatuses have dominated black America. In agricultural slavery beginning in the early eighteenth century, black America was constituted (via ideological apparatuses, i.e., church, slave quarters, juke-joints, and the so-called big house of the plantations) as a racial caste in class dominated by the social class language game of the black bourgeoisie (E. Franklin Frazier's term), the best of the house servants, artisans, and free blacks from the North under the leadership of black Protestant male preachers, which discriminated against the practical consciousness and linguistic system (social class language games) of field slaves and newly arrived Africans, working in agricultural production, who constituted the black underclass. As such, Black English Vernacular emerged among the field slaves whose way of life was juxtaposed against house slaves who identified and patterned their ways of dress, speech, and religiosity after their-white slavemasters of the church and the "big house" (Frazier, 1936).

Deagriculturalization and the industrialization of the northern states coupled with black American migration to the north from the mid-1800s to about the mid-1950s, gave rise to the continual racial-class separation between this urban, educated, and professional class of blacks and former house slaves whose practical consciousness and linguistic system mirrored that of middle class whites, and a Black English speaking black underclass of former agricultural workers seeking, like their black bourgeois counterparts, to be bourgeois, i.e., economic gain, status, and upward economic mobility, through education and industrial work in Northern cities. However, racial discrimination coupled with suburbanization and the deindustrialization, or outsourcing of industrial work to Third World countries, of northern cities left the majority of blacks as part of the poor black underclass with limited occupational and educational opportunities (Wilson, 1978, 1987). As such, prisons, the streets, athletics, and the entertainment industry became the dominant ideological apparatuses of the inner-cities. Consequently, contemporarily, America's transition from an industrial base to a postindustrial, financialized service, economy beginning in the 1970s positioned black American underclass ideology and language, hip-hop culture, as constituted via the streets, prisons, athletics and entertainment industries, as a viable means for black American youth to achieve economic gain, status, and upward economic mobility in the society over education. That is, finance capital in the US beginning in the 1970s began investing in entertainment and other service industries where the segregated inner-city street, prison, language, entertainment, and athletic culture of black America became both a commodity and the means to economic gain for the black poor in America's postindustrial economy, which subsequently outsourced its industrial work to semi-periphery nations thereby blighting the inner-city communities.

Blacks, many of whom migrated to the northern cities from the agricultural south looking for industrial work in the north, became concentrated and segregated in blighted communities where work began to disappear, schools were under funded, and poverty and crime increased due to deindustrialization and suburbanization of northern cities (Wilson, 1993, 1987, 1978). As such, poorly-funded schools, the streets, police officers, and prisons became the dominant ideological apparatuses of their communities. The black migrants, which migrated North with their BEV/AAEV from the agricultural South following the Civil War and later, became segregated sociolinguistic underclass communities, ghettoes, of unemployed laborers looking to illegal, athletic, and entertainment activities (running numbers, pimping, prostitution, drug dealing, robbing, participating in sports, music, etc.) for economic success, status, and upward mobility. Educated in the poorly funded schools of the urban ghettoes, given the process of deindustrialization and the flight of capital to the suburbs and overseas, with no work prospects, many black Americans became part of a permanent *social class language game*, AAEV speaking and poorly educated underclass looking to other activities for economic gain, status, and upward economic mobility. Those who were educated, became successful athletically, and through the entertainment industry became a part of the Standard-English-speaking black middle class of professionals, i.e., teachers, doctors, lawyers, etc. (the black bourgeoisie), living in the suburbs, while the uneducated or poorly educated constituted the black underclass of the urban ghettoes looking to illegal activities for economic-gain, upward mobility, and success. Beginning in the late 1980s, finance capital, in order to avoid the oppositional culture to poverty, racism, and classism found among the black underclass, began commodifying and distributing (via the media industrial complex) the underclass black practical consciousness, constituted by the streets, prisons, the athletic and entertainment industries, for entertainment in the emerging postindustrial service economy of the US over the ideology and language of the black bourgeoisie. Be that as it may, efforts to succeed academically among black Americans, which constituted the ideology and language of the black bourgeoisie, paled in comparison to their efforts to succeed as speakers of Black English, athletes, "gangstas," "playas," and entertainers, which became the ideology and language of the black underclass urban youth living in the inner-cities of America. Authentic black American identity became synonymous with black American underclass hip-hop ideology and language as financed by the upper-class of owners and high-level executives of the entertainment industry over the social class language game of the educated and church-attending black middle class.

Hence, contemporarily, in America's postindustrial service economy where multiculturalism, language, and communication skills, pedagogically taught through process approaches to learning, multicultural education, and cooperative group works in school, are keys to succeeding in the postindustrial service labor market, blacks, paradoxically, have an advantage and disadvantage. On the one hand, their linguistic structure growing up in inner-cities are influenced by the black American underclass who in conjunction with the upper-class of owners and high-level executives have positioned athletics and the entertainment industries as the social functions best served by their linguistic structure in the service economy of the US, which subsequently leads to economic gain, status, and upward social mobility for young urban blacks in the society. This is advantageous because it becomes an authentic black identity by which black American youth can participate in the fabric of the postindustrial social structure. On the other hand, their linguistic structure inhibits them from succeeding academically given the mismatch between their linguistic structure and the function it serves in the postindustrial labor market of the US, and that of Standard English and the function of school as a medium to economic gain, status, and upward social mobility for blacks in the society.

School for many black Americans, especially black boys, in other words, is simply a place for honing their athletic and entertainment skills and hip-hop culture, which they can subsequently profit from in the American postindustrial service economy as their cultural contribution to the American multicultural melting pot. Many black American youth of the inner-cities enter school speaking Black or African American English Vernacular. Their linguistic structure in schooling in postindustrial education, which values the exchange of cultural facts as commodities for the postindustrial economy, is celebrated along with their music and athletics under the umbrella of multicultural education. Therefore, no, or very few, remedial courses are offered to teach them Standard English, which initially leads to poor test scores on standardized tests because the phonology, morphology, and syntax, or the way its expressions are put together to form sentences, of BEV/AAEV juxtaposed against that of Standard English (SE) linguistically prevents many black Americans from the inner-cities early on in their academic careers from grasping the meaning or semantics of phrases and contents of standardized tests, which are written in Standard English. As blacks matriculate through the school system, with their emphasis of succeeding in music and athletics, those who acquire the systemicity of Standard English and succeed become part of the black professional class celebrating the underclass culture, from whence they came, of those who do not make it and therefore dropout of school constituting the black underclass of poorly educated and unemployed social actors looking to the entertainment industry (which celebrates their conditions as a commodity for the labor market) and the streets as their only viable means to economic gain, status, and upward social mobility in blighted inner-city communities.

Hence American blacks, as interpellated (workers) and embourgeoised agents of the American postindustrial capitalist social structure of inequality, represent the most modern (i.e. socialized) people of color, in terms of their "practical consciousness," in the process of homogenizing social actors as agents of the protestant ethic or disciplined workers, producers, and consumers working for owners of production in order to obtain economic gain, status, and upward mobility in the larger American society (Frazier, 1957; Wilson, 1978; Glazer and Moynihan, 1963; Mocombe, 2009). They constitute the American social space in terms of their relation to the means of production in post-industrial capitalist America and its ideological apparatuses, which differentiates black America for the most part into two status groups or social class language games, a dwindling middle and upper class (living in suburbia) that numbers about 25 percent of their population (13 percent) and obtain their status as doctors, athletes, entertainers, lawyers, teachers, and other high-end professional service occupations; and a growing segregated "black underclass" of unemployed and under-employed wage-earners, gangsters, rappers, and athletes occupying poor inner-city communities and schools focused solely on technical skills, multicultural education, athletics, and test-taking for social promotion given the relocation (outsourcing) of industrial and manufacturing jobs to poor periphery and semi-periphery countries and the introduction of low-end post-industrial service jobs and a growing informal economy in American urban-cities. Consequently, the poor performance of black American students, vis-à-vis whites, in education as an ideological apparatus for this post-industrial capitalist sociolinguistic worldview leaves them disproportionately in this growing underclass of laborers, rappers, gangsters, athletes, and entertainers at the bottom of the American postindustrial class social structure of inequality unable to either transform their world as they encounter it, or truly exercise their embourge-oisement given their lack of, what sociologist Pierre Bourdieu (1973, 1984) refers to as, capital (cultural, social, economic, and political).

Contrary to John Ogbu's (1986) burden of acting white hypothesis, it is due to their indigent (pathological-pathogenic) structural position within the American capitalist social structure of inequality, as opposed to a differing or oppositional cultural ethos from that of the latter, as to the reason why black American school children underachieve vis-à-vis their white counterparts. That is, the majority of black American school students underachieve in school in general and on standardized test in particular, vis-à-vis their white counterparts, not because they possess or are taught (by their peers) at an early age distinct normative cultural values from that of the dominant group of owners and high-level executives in the social structure that transfer into cultural and political conflict in the classroom as an ideological apparatus for capitalists. To the contrary, black American students underachieve in school because in acquiring the "verbal behavior" of the dominant powers of the social structure in segregated "poor" gentrified inner-city communities which lack good legal jobs and affordable resources that have been outsourced by capital overseas (outsourcing), the majority, who happen to be less educated in the "Standard English" of the society, have reinforced a linguistic (Black English Vernacular) community or status group of gangstas, rappers, athletes, and entertainers, the black underclass, as the bearers of ideological and linguistic domination for black America, whose practices have been commodified by finance capital to accumulate surplus-value in their postindustrial economy (Mocombe, 2006, 2011).

It is this "mismatch of linguistic social class function," role conflict, the ideals of middle class black and white bourgeois America against the perceived "pathologies" (functions) of the black underclass, reproduced via ideological apparatuses such as the streets, prisons, the media, the athletic and entertainment industries, etc., as a sociolinguistic status group in the American postindustrial class social structure of inequality, Ogbu and other post-segregationist black middle-class scholars inappropriately label, "acting-white," "culture of poverty," or oppositional culture. Blacks, boys in particular, are neither concealing their academic prowess and abilities when they focus, and defer their efforts, on the street life, athletics, music, entertainment, etc. for fear of acting white as Ogbu suggests, nor do they internalize residual white stereotypes of a remote past. Instead, they are focusing on racially coded socioeconomic actions or roles commodified in the larger American postindustrial capitalist social structure of inequality that are more likely to lead to economic gain, status, prestige, and upward mobility in the society as defined for, and by, the black underclass financed by finance capital.

The black underclass youth in America's ghettoes has slowly become, since the 1980s, with the financialization of hip-hop culture by record labels such as Sony and others, athletics, and the entertainment industry, the bearers of ideological and linguistic domination for the black community in America. Their language and worldview as constituted through prisons, the streets, hip-hop culture, athletics and the entertainment industry financed by finance capital, and reproduced via ideological apparatuses such as the streets, prisons, schools, and the media has become the means by which many black youth (and youth throughout the world) attempt to recursively reorganize and reproduce their material resource framework against the purposive-rationality of black bourgeois or middle class America. The upper-class of owners and high-level executives of the American dominated capitalist world-system have capitalized on this through the commodification of black underclass culture. This is further supported by an American media and popular culture that glorifies athletes, entertainers, and the "Bling bling," wealth, diamonds, cars, jewelry, and money of the culture. Hence the aim of many young black people, black males in particular, in the society is no longer to seek status, economic gain, and upward mobility through a Protestant Ethic that stresses hard work, diligence, differed gratification, and education; on the contrary, a Protestant Ethic that stresses hard work in sports, music, instant gratification, illegal activities (drug dealing), and skimming are the dominant means portrayed for their efforts through the entertainment industry financed by post-industrial capital. Schools throughout urban American inner cities are no longer seen as means to a professional end in order to obtain economic gain, status, and upward mobility, but obstacles to that end because it delays gratification and is not correlative with the means, social roles and ideological apparatuses, associated with economic success and upward mobility in black urban underclass America. More black American youth (especially the black male) want to become, gangstas, football and basketball players, rappers and entertainers, like many of their role models who were raised in their underclass environments and obtained economic gain and upward mobility that way, over pastors, doctors, lawyers, engineers, etc., the social functions associated with the status symbol of the black and white middle professional (educated) class of the civil rights generation. Hence the end and social action remains the same, economic success, status, and upward economic mobility, only the means to that end have shifted with the rise, financed by finance capital, of the black underclass as the bearers of ideological and linguistic domination in black America given the commodification of hip-hop culture and their high visibility in the media and charitable works through basketball and football camps and rap concerts, which reinforce the aforementioned activities as viable means to wealth and status in the society's postindustrial economy, which focuses on services and entertainment for the world's transnational bourgeois class as the mode of producing surplus-value.

This linguistic and ideological domination and the ends of the power elites (rappers, athletes, gangsters) of the black underclass, "mismatch of linguistic structure and social function," which brings about the role conflict Ogbu interprets as the burden of acting white, are juxtaposed against the Protestant Ethic and spirit of capitalism of the black middle and upper middle educated and church-attending professional classes represented in the prosperity discourse and discursive practices of black American preachers in the likes of Michael Eric Dyson, TD Jakes, Creflo Dollar, Eddie Long, etc. who push forth, via the black American church, education, and professional jobs as viable means to prosperity, status, and upward economic gain. Hence, whereas, for agents of the Protestant Ethic and the spirit of capitalism in the likes of Dyson, Jakes, Dollar, Eddie Long, and Juanita Bynum the means to "Bling bling," or the American Dream, is through education and obtaining a professional job as a sign of God's grace and salvation, Rapping, hustling, sports, etc., for younger black Americans growing up in gentrified inner-cities throughout the US, where industrial work has disappeared, represent the means (not education) to the status position of "Bling bling." So what we are suggesting here is that contemporarily many black youth are not "acting white" when education no longer becomes a priority or the means to economic gain, status, and upward mobility, as they get older and consistently underachieve vis-à-vis whites; they are attempting to be white and achieve bourgeois economic status (the "Bling bling" of cars, diamonds, gold, helicopters, money, etc.) in the society by being "black," speaking Ebonics, rapping, playing sports, hustling, etc., in a racialized post-industrial capitalist social structure wherein the economic status of "blackness" is (over) determined by the white capitalists class of owners and high-level executives and the black proletariats of the West, the black underclass, whose way of life and image ("athletes, hustlers, hip-hopsters") has been commodified (by white and black capitalists) and distributed throughout the world for entertainment, (black) status, and economic purposes in post-industrial capitalist America. This underclass culture as globally promulgated to urban black youth throughout the black diaspora by finance capital via Black Entertainment Television (BET) and other media outlets is counterbalanced or opposed by black preachers promoting the same ethos, The Protestant Ethic and the spirit of capitalism, via the prosperity gospel, patriarchy, misogyny, etc., of the black American churches, to the black administrative bourgeoisie around the world via biblical conversion or salvation, over the so-called pathologies, promiscuity, misogyny, patriarchy, etc., of the black American underclass, as the medium to and for success in the capitalist world-system. Hence, the social structure of class (not racial or cultural worldview) inequality that characterizes the black American social environment is subsequently the relational framework, which black youth and the black administrative bourgeoisie in America and the diaspora are exposed to and socialized in when they encounter globalizing processes through immigration, the outsourcing of work from America, and the images of the entertainment industry and black church. Throughout America, the continent of Africa, the Caribbean, and black Europe black American charismatic preachers are promoting a prosperity gospel among the black poor and administrative bourgeoisie, which is usually juxtaposed against the emergence of an underclass culture among the youth in these areas influenced by the hip-hop and athletic culture of the black American underclass (Ntarangwi, 2009).

The aforementioned processes, as Mocombe and Tomlin (2013) demonstrates, is clearly evidenced among black British Caribbean youth in the United Kingdom whose experiences parallel that of black Americans in the United States. As such, like the black Americans in the US, the underachievement of black British Caribbean youths is tied to this mismatch of linguistic structure and social class function, which is an epiphenomenon of the capitalist social structure of class inequality and its ideological apparatuses. Like black America, two social class language games emerged in the Caribbean as a result of the capitalist social relations of production and its ideological apparatuses.

In the Caribbean, most ex-slaves participated in local affairs only marginally more than East Indians during colonialism. In the French and British Caribbean, for instance, whites controlled the local legislature with a handful of men of color who were ideologically and linguistically interpellated and embourgeoised as middle class administrators of the colonial system. The twentieth and twenty-first centuries witnessed a shift in the power in the Caribbean following the end of the colonial system, however. Black and other people of color increased their influence in government and other institutions under the middle class or European influences (embourgeoisement) of the handful of men of color who once ruled with whites during colonialism. Although, the relationship between blacks and whites changed, the continued separation of the black majority from the white and brown minorities meant the poor, who were mainly blacks, developed their own underclass patterns of behavior and beliefs, ideologies and linguistic structures, which became juxtaposed against the middle class and European identities of those in power. Education in the Caribbean, for the most part continued to be an elite privilege. The poor constituted a poorly educated underclass living either in the overcrowded Caribbean capital cities or small farm towns, looking to immigrate to the homeland of their former colonial masters for work and better economic opportunities. The well-to-do, for the most part, paid for private, parochial education; upon completion, they subsequently sent their children abroad for secondary schooling. In many instances, they returned back to the islands where they assumed administrative and bureaucratic roles in government or the private sector. Hence Caribbean society, as well as its immigration pattern overseas, would become juxtaposed between, or against, the poorly educated underclass speakers of Creole or Caribbean patois and an embourgeoised middle class of non-white administrators who, contemporarily, served the same purpose as the handful of colored persons who administered the islands with whites during the colonial period. Be that as it may, upon immigration to places like the UK, racism in the labor, housing, and educational markets, which paralleled what happened to the black American in the US, segregated the majority of the black Caribbean immigrants seeking to achieve the embourgeoisement of their former colonial masters in poor gentrified communities. What developed then was a caste, color, and class system in places like the UK in which the black immigrants sought the embourgeoisement of their former colonial masters through education in segregated poor black communities where work was beginning to disappear to the suburbs or overseas, while simultaneously reproducing a class system in which those who did not attain the middle class ideology and language of the former colonial masters constituted an underclass of poorly educated, unemployed, and patois speaking blacks looking to hustling, the entertainment industry, and sports as viable means to status and upward economic mobility in the UK's emerging postindustrial economy.

Ostensibly, influenced by the success and overrepresentation of the black American underclass, who positioned, with the help of finance capital, their underclass culture as viable means to economic gain, status, and upward mobility in America and the global marketplace, black British youth have sought to do the same as they positioned black British Talk (BBT) and underclass practices, hustling, participating in sports and the entertainment industry, as means or social class roles to status in Britain and the global marketplaces over and against the educational orientation of the black British and American middle classes of earlier generations who did not perceive their embourgeoisement attained via the church and education as the status markers of whites. This has led, as in the case of the black American, to the academic underachievement of black British Caribbean youth due to two factors, a mismatch of linguistic structure (mismatch between black British Talk and Standard British English) when they initially enter school, and later on due to a mismatch of linguistic social class function as they do not apply themselves to academically achieve because of the disconnect between their linguistic structure (black British Talk) and economic success for blacks in the UK and global marketplaces.

Globally, more blacks, of any nationality, are over-represented in the media as having achieved status and upward economic mobility speaking their patois, hustling, playing sports, and entertaining than achieving academically and speaking the *lingua franca* of the power elites. As a result, blacks, black males in particular, are less likely to identify with or place much effort into education, unlike their female counterparts, as a viable means to economic gain, status, and upward mobility in a global marketplace under US hegemony dominated by images of successful black males as hustlers, athletes, and entertainers, social class roles black females are less likely to achieve status, economic gain, or upward economic mobility in. As such, it is within this class dialectic that the black male/female intra-racial gender academic achievement gap in the US and the UK emerged and must be framed and studied.

Within Mocombe's "mismatch of linguistic structure and social class function" hypothesis, the theoretical assumption is that the black male/female intra-racial gender academic achievement gap is a result of the social class functions associated with the urban street life of postindustrial America and the United Kingdom where black males predominantly achieve their status, social mobility, and economic gain, and the black church where black females achieve their status, social mobility, and drive for economic gain via education and technical professionalization. In other words, as many black males of the urban cities in the US and UK sought to achieve economic gain, status, and upward social mobility via athletics, entertainment, and the street life, which led to high school dropout, criminality, and murder rates in the urban inner-cities of postindustrial America and the United Kingdom beginning in the 1980s, their efforts to achieve academically was superseded by their efforts to succeed via the streets, the entertainment, and athletic industries of industrial and postindustrial America where they became embraced by the larger society and the black upper/middle class of professionals. Conversely, given the limited opportunities afforded to black women by the athletic and entertainment industries and the urban street life, they turned to the black church where they found solace from the murder rates and criminality of the cities. Within the church, they encountered a prosperity gospel under the leadership of black educated professional women and men and black charismatic Protestant preachers in the likes of TD Jakes, Creflo Dollar, Eddie Long, Juanita Bynum, etc., promoting the same status, economic gain, and upward economic mobility of black urban America and the United Kingdom via the status associated with the church, education, and technical professionalization against the misogyny and patriarchy of the street, athletic, and entertainment culture of black urban hip-hop America. As a result, black females, who are grossly over-represented in black churches predominantly under the leadership of black male preachers, were more likely to place emphasis on achieving economic gain, status, and upward economic mobility via the church, as prophetesses, evangelists, etc., education, and technical professionalization over the streets, athletic and entertainment industries where their opportunities were limited by young black males who relegated them to dancers and groupies in hip-hop music videos. As such, black womanhood became defined by black educated and professional females who attended church regularly, spoke standard American English, and better off than those females represented by their depiction in hip-hop music videos and the street-life, who spoke Black English Vernacular. The former esteemed more than the latter.

Hence it is due to a mismatch of linguistic social class function within the dialectical class dynamic of black America and the United Kingdom that the intra-racial gender academic achievement gap emerged and must be understood. Black females given their limited opportunities in the streets, entertainment, and athletic culture of post-industrial America and the United Kingdom were, and are, more likely to place their efforts on achieving status, economic gain, and upward social mobility via the church, where education and technical professionalization are stressed over the lifestyles of the urban street life in both countries. They became church attending, Standard English speaking, and educated professionals, who discriminated against their street counterparts, who were less educated, Black English Vernacular speaking, and non-church attending members associated with the street life of urban America where they are depicted as "bitches" and "hoes." The Protestant Church culture of blacks in America and the United Kingdom marginalized the latter and their black male counterparts.

Just as in the case of less educated, Black English Vernacular speaking, and non-church attending black female members, the black church marginalized black males because of their prosperity gospel which discriminated against poorly educated and jobless black males, who turned to the streets, athletics, and the entertainment industries for their status, upward economic mobility, and economic gain. The black males who achieved status, economic gain, and upward economic mobility in the larger society returned to the black church where their economic positions made them social role models for the few black males in the church.

The black Church, as such, became and is constituted between black females, who achieved their status, economic gain, and upward economic mobility via education, and black males who achieved their status as athletes, entertainers, and a few who achieved it via education. Both groups discriminate against what is deemed as the pathologies, cursing, street and prison life, speaking Black English, promiscuity, etc., of the black male and female underclass. The black male athletes and entertainers, as in the larger mainstream media, dominate leadership positions in the church given their status, serving, along with the preachers and deacons, as role models for the few black males in the church. Their status positions are normally professionalized and juxtaposed against black males from the streets whose representations as "thugs," "pimps," and "hoods" in hip-hop music videos are marginalized against in the church culture of the former and the educated black females, who look down upon their black female underclass counterparts.

Future research must explore both the black/white academic achievement gap and the intra-racial black male/female gender academic achievement gap within the framework of Mocombe's structural Marxist "mismatch of linguistic structure and social class function" hypothesis through assessment of black test scores vis-à-vis their linguistic structure; survey-based research assessing the career goals of young blacks, men and women; and the influence of black American underclass lifestyle and culture in the black diaspora, what Mocombe refers to the African-Americanization of the black diaspora. So long as blacks in America, the United Kingdom, and elsewhere insist on reproducing the Protestant Ethic and the spirit of capitalism of their former slavemasters and colonizers, the black/white academic achievement gap will remain among us.

Chapter Five

Jesus and the Streets

Jesus and the streets represent two metaphors that highlight the dominant ideological apparatuses, the church/schools and the streets/prison life, respectively, wherein black females and males are interpellated and socialized in the American and British capitalist social structure of racial-class inequality. Within Mocombe's "mismatch of linguistic structure and social class function" hypothesis, the theoretical assumption is that the black male/female intra-racial gender academic achievement gap is a result of the social class functions associated with the urban street and prison life of postindustrial America and the United Kingdom where black males predominantly achieve their status, social mobility, and economic gain, and the black church where black females achieve their status, social mobility, and drive for economic gain via education and technical professionalization. In other words, as many black males of the urban cities in the US and UK sought to achieve economic gain, status, and upward social mobility via athletics, entertainment, and the street life, which led to high school dropout, criminality, and murder rates in the urban inner-cities of postindustrial America and the United Kingdom beginning in the 1980s, their efforts to achieve academically was superseded by their efforts to succeed via the streets, the entertainment, and athletic industries of industrial and postindustrial America where they became embraced by the larger society and the black upper/middle class of professionals. Conversely, given the limited opportunities afforded to black women by the athletic and entertainment industries and the urban street life, they turned to the black church where they found solace from the murder rates and criminality of the cities. Within the church, they encountered a prosperity gospel under the leadership of black educated professional women and men and black charismatic Protestant preachers in the likes of TD Jakes, Creflo Dollar, Eddie Long, Juanita Bynum, etc., promoting the same status,

economic gain, and upward economic mobility of black urban America and
the United Kingdom via the status associated with the church, education, and
technical professionalization against the misogyny and patriarchy of the
street, athletic, and entertainment culture of black urban hip-hop America. As
a result, black females, who are grossly over-represented in black churches
predominantly under the leadership of black male preachers, were more likely to place emphasis on achieving economic gain, status, and upward economic mobility via the church, as prophetesses, evangelists, etc., education,
and technical professionalization over the streets, athletic and entertainment
industries where their opportunities were limited by young black males who
relegated them to dancers and groupies in hip-hop music videos. As such,
black womanhood became defined by black women on the one hand by black
educated and professional females who attended church regularly, spoke
standard American English, and better off than those females represented by
their depiction in hip-hop music videos and the street-life, who spoke black
English Vernacular. The former esteemed more than the latter.

Hence it is due to a mismatch of linguistic social class function within the
dialectical class dynamic of black America and the United Kingdom that the
intra-racial gender academic achievement gap emerged and must be understood. Black females given their limited opportunities in the streets, entertainment, and athletic culture of post-industrial America and the United
Kingdom were and are more likely to place their efforts on achieving status,
economic gain, and upward social mobility via the church, where education
and technical professionalization are stressed over the lifestyles of the urban
street life in both countries. They became church attending, Standard English
speaking, and educated professionals, who discriminated against their street
counterparts, who were less educated, Black English Vernacular speaking,
and non-church attending members associated with the street life of urban
America where they are depicted as "bitches" and "hoes." The Protestant
Church culture of blacks in America and the United Kingdom marginalized
the latter and their black male counterparts.

Just as in the case of less educated, Black English Vernacular speaking,
and non-church attending black female members, the black church marginalized black males because of their prosperity gospel which discriminated
against poorly educated and jobless black males, who turned to the streets,
athletics, and the entertainment industries for their status, upward economic
mobility, and economic gain. The black males who achieved status, economic gain, and upward economic mobility in the larger society returned to the
black church where their economic positions made them social role models
for the few black males in the church.

The black Church, as such, became and is constituted between black
females, who achieved their status, economic gain, and upward economic
mobility via education, and black males who achieved their status as athletes,

entertainers, and a few who achieved it via education. Both groups discriminate against what is deemed as the pathologies, cursing, speaking Black English, promiscuity, etc., of the black male and female underclass. The black male athletes and entertainers, as in the larger mainstream media, dominate leadership positions in the church given their status, serving, along with the preachers and deacons, as role models for the few black males in the church. Their status positions are normally professionalized and juxtaposed against black males from the streets whose representations as "thugs," "pimps," and "hoods" in hip-hop music videos are marginalized against in the church culture of the former and the educated black females, who look down upon their black female underclass counterparts.

Future research must explore both the black/white academic achievement gap and the intra-racial black male/female gender academic achievement gap within the framework of Mocombe's structural Marxist "mismatch of linguistic structure and social class function" hypothesis through assessment of black test scores vis-à-vis their linguistic structure; survey-based research assessing the career goals of young blacks; and the influence of black American underclass lifestyle and culture on the black diaspora, what Mocombe refers to as the African-Americanization of the black diaspora. In the end, our recommendation is not for black leadership to coerce more black males to attend church like their female counterparts over adopting the street, prison, athletic, and entertainment culture of the urban cities. On the contrary, the emphasis should be on untangling the ideological apparatuses, the church, education, prisons, etc., of society from capitalists and the mode of production, and orienting them towards the universe and our relations to it and the earth!

References Cited

Abbas, S. British South Asians and Pathways into Selective Schooling: Social Class, Culture and Ethnicity (2007) *British Educational Research Journal* 33 (1): 75–90.

Ackroyd, P. (2001) *London the Biography*. London: Vintage.

Adorno, Theodor W. (2000). *Negative Dialectics*. New York: Continuum.

Allen, Ernest Jr. (2002). "Du Boisian Double Consciousness: The Unsustainable Argument." *The Massachusetts Review*, 43 (2): 217–253.

Allen, Ernest Jr. (1992). "Ever Feeling One's Twoness: 'Double Ideals and 'Double Consciousness' in the Souls of Black Folk." *Critique of Anthropology*, 12 (3): 261–275.

Allen, Richard L. (2001). *The Concept of Self: A Study of Black Identity and Self Esteem.* Detroit: Wayne State University Press.

Alleyne, M. (1980). *Comparative Afro-American*. Ann Arbor: Karoman Press. (1989) *The Roots of Jamaican Culture* . London: Pluto Press.

Althusser, Louis (2001). *Lenin and Philosophy and Other Essays*. New York: Monthly Review Press.

Althusser, Louis and Étienne Balibar (1970). *Reading Capital* (Ben Brewster, Trans.). London: NLB.

Altschuler, Richard (ed.) (1998). *The living Legacy of Marx, Durkheim, and Weber: Applications and Analyses of Classical Sociological Theory by Modern Social Scientists.* New York: Gordian Knot Books.

Appiah, Anthony (1985). "The Uncompleted Argument: Du Bois and the Illusion of Race." *Critical Inquiry*, 12: 21–37.

Aptheker, Herbert (ed.) (1985). *W.E.B. Du Bois Against Racism: Unpublished Essays, Papers, Addresses, 1887–1961.* Amherst: The University of Massachusetts Press.

Archer, L. (2003) *Race, Masculinity and Schooling: Muslim Boys and Education.* Maidenhead: Open University Press.

Archer, L. (2009) The 'Black' Middle classes and Education: Parents and Young People's Constructions of Identity, Values and Educational Practices. Paper Presented to British Education Research Association (BERA) September. University of Manchester.

Archer, L. (2011) Constructing Minority Ethnic Middle-class identity: An Exploratory Study with Parents, Pupils and Young Professionals. *Sociology* 45 (1): 134–151.

Archer, L. & Francis, B. (2007) *Understanding Minority Ethnic Achievement: Race, Gender, Class and 'Success'*. London: Routledge.

Archer, Margaret S. (1985). "Structuration versus Morphogenesis." In H.J. Helle and S.N. Eisenstadt (Eds.), *Macro-Sociological Theory: Perspectives on Sociological Theory* (Volume 1) (pp. 58–88). United Kingdom: J.W. Arrowsmith Ltd.

Arnot, M., David, M and Weiner, G. (1996). *Recent Research on Gender and Educational Performance*. London: HMSO.

Asante, Molefi Kete (1988). *Afrocentricity*. New Jersey: Africa World.

Asante, Molefi K. (1990a). *Kemet, Afrocentricity and Knowledge*. New Jersey: Africa World.

Asante, Molefi K. (1990b). "African Elements in African-American English." In Joseph E. Holloway (Ed.), *Africanisms in American Culture* (pp. 19–33). Bloomington and Indianapolis: Indiana University Press.

Austin, J.L. (1997). *How to do Things With Words* (Second edition, J.O. Urmson and Marina Sbisà, editors). Cambridge, Massachusetts: Harvard University Press.

Bailey, B.L. (1966). *Jamaican Creole Syntax*. Cambridge: Cambridge University Press.

Baker, Houston A., Jr. (1985). "The Black Man of Culture: W.E.B. Du Bois and The Souls of Black Folk." In William L. Andrews (Ed.), *Critical Essays on W.E.B. Du Bois* (pp.129–139). Boston: G.K. Hall & Co.

Balibar, Etienne & Immanuel Wallerstein (1991 [1988]). *Race, Nation, Class: Ambiguous Identities*. London: Verso.

Ballantine, Jeanne, H. (1993). *The Sociology of Education: A systematic Analysis* (3rd Edition). New Jersey: Prentice Hall.

Ball, Howard (2000). *The Bakke Case: Race, Education, and Affirmative Action*. Kansas: University Press of Kansas.

Barone, C. (2006). Cultural Capital, Ambition and the Explanation of Inequalities in Learning Outcomes: A Comparative Analysis. *Sociology*, 40 (6): 1039–1058.

Barrs, M. and Cork, V. (2001). *The Reader in the Writer: The Links between the Study of Literature and Writing Development at Key Stage 2*. London: Centre for Language in Primary Education.

Barthes, Roland (1972). *Mythologies* (Annette Lavers, Trans.). New York: Hill and Wang.

Bashi, V and Hughes, M. (1997) Globalization and Residential Segregation by 'Race.' *Annuls of the American Academy of Social and Political Science*, 551: 105–20.

Bell, Daniel (1985). *The Social Sciences Since the Second World War*. New Brunswick (USA): Transaction Books.

Bell, Bernard W. et al (editors) (1996). *W. E. B. Du Bois on Race and Culture: Philosophy, Politics, and Poetics*. New York and London: Routledge.

Bell, Bernard W. (1996). "Genealogical Shifts in Du Bois's Discourse on Double Consciousness as the Sign of African American Difference." In Bernard W. Bell et al (Eds.), *W.E.B. Du Bois on Race and Culture: Philosophy, Politics, and Poetics* (pp. 87–108). New York and London: Routledge.

Bell, Bernard W. (1985). "W.E.B. Du Bois's Struggle to Reconcile Folk and High Art." In William L. Andrews (Ed.), *Critical Essays on W.E.B. Du Bois* (pp.106–122). Andrews. Boston: G.K. Hall & Co.

Bearne, E. (Ed). (1998). *Language across the Curriculum*. London: Routledge.

Bennett, Lerone (1982). *Before the Mayflower*. Chicago: Johnson Publishing Company .

Bernstein, B. (1971*) Class, Codes and Control*. New York: Schocken Books.

Berthoud, R. (2000) Ethnic Employment Penalties in Britain. *Journal of Ethnic and Migration Studies*. 26 (3): pp. 389–416.

Berthoud (2009) 'Patterns of Non-employment, and of Disadvantage, in a Recession', Working Paper No. 2009–23, Institute for Social and Economic Research, University of Essex. http://www.ippr.org/uploadedFiles/events/Youth%20unemployment%20and%20recession%20technical%20briefing.pdf Accessed on Wednesday October 12, 2011.

Bhabha, Homi (1995a). "Cultural Diversity and Cultural Differences." In Bill Ashcroft et al (Eds.), *The Post-colonial Studies Reader* (pp. 206–209). London and New York: Routledge.

Bhabha, Homi (1995b). "Signs Taken for Wonders." In Bill Ashcroft et al (Eds.), *The Post-colonial Studies Reader* (pp. 29–35). London and New York: Routledge.

Bhabha, Homi (1994). "Remembering Fanon: Self, Psyche and the Colonial Condition." In Patrick Williams and Laura Chrisman (Eds.), *Colonial Discourse and Post-Colonial Theory A Reader* (pp. 112–123). New York: Columbia University Press.

Bhattacharyya, G., Ison, L. & Blair, M. (2003) *Minority Ethnic Attainment and Participation in Education and Training: the Evidence.* DFES RTPOl-03: London.
Bickerton, D. (1975). *Dynamics of a Creole System.* Cambridge: Cambridge University Press.
Billingsley, Andrew (1968). *Black Families in White America.* New Jersey: Prentice Hall.
Billingsley, Andrew (1970). "Black Families and White Social Science." *Journal of Social Issues,* 26, 127–142.
Billingsley, Andrew (1993). *Climbing Jacob's Ladder: The Enduring Legacy of African American Families.* New York: Simon & Schuster.
Birmingham Economic Information Centre. http://www.birminghameconomy.org.uk/sum/ kfsumgcse.htm Accessed on Thursday February 21, 2008.
Bizzell, Patricia and Bruce Herzberg (2001). *The Rhetorical Tradition: Readings from Classical Times to the Present.* Boston: Bedford/St. Martin's.
Blackaby, D.H, Leslie, D.G.& Murphy, :D. (2005) N. C. O'Leary Born in Britain: How Are Native Ethnic Minorities faring in the British Labor Market? *Economic Letters* 88 (3): 370–375.
Blair, M. (2001b) *Why Pick on Me: School Exclusion and Black Youth.* Stoke-on Trent: Trentham Books.
Blassingame, John W. (1972). *The Slave Community: Plantation Life in the Antebellum South.* New York: Oxford University Press.
Bleich, E. (2003) *Race and Politics in Britain and France: Ideas and Policy-making since the 1960s.* Cambridge: Cambridge University Press.
Boskin, Joseph (1965). "Race Relations in Seventeenth-Century America: The Problem of the Origins of Negro Slavery." In Donald Noel (Ed.), *The Origins of American Slavery and Racism* (pp. 95–105). Ohio: Charles E. Merrill Publishing Co.
Boswell, Terry (1989). "Colonial Empires and the Capitalist World-Economy: A Time Series Analysis of Colonization, 1640–1960." *American Sociological Review,* 54, 180–196.
Bourdieu, Pierre (1984). *Distinction: A Social Critique of the Judgement of Taste* (Richard Nice, Trans.). Cambridge MA: Harvard University Press.
Bourdieu, P. (1986). The Forms of Capital. In J.E. Richardson (Ed.), *Handbook of Theory and Research for the Sociology of Education* (pp. 241–258). Westport: Greenwood Press.
Bourdieu, Pierre (1990). *The Logic of Practice* (Richard Nice, Trans.). Stanford, California: Stanford University Press.
Boxill, Bernard R. (1996). "Du Bois on Cultural Pluralism." In Bell W. Bernard et al (Eds.), *W.E.B. Du Bois on Race and Culture: Philosophy, Politics, and Poetics* (pp. 57–86). New York and London: Routledge.
Brathwaite, E. (1984). *History of the Voice.* London: New Beacon Books.
Brecher, Jeremy and Tim Costello (1998). *Global Village or Global Pillage: Economic Reconstruction from the bottom up* (second ed.). Cambridge, Mass.: South End Press.
Brennan, Teresa (1997). "The Two Forms of Consciousness." *Theory Culture & Society,* 14 (4): 89–96.
Broderick, Francis L. (1959). *W.E.B. Du Bois, Negro Leader in a Time of Crisis.* Stanford, California: Stanford University Press.
Brown, C. (1985) *Black and White Britain.* London: Policy Studies Institute.
Bruce, Dickinson D., Jr. (1992). "W.E.B. Du Bois and the Idea of Double Consciousness." *American Literature,* 64: 299–309.
Bryan, B. (1982). Language, dialect and identity: An examination of the writing of bi-dialectal adults in a London FE college. Unpublished MA thesis, Institute of Education, University of London.
Bryan, B. (1998). A comparison of approaches to teaching English in two sociolinguistic environments (Jamaica and London). Unpublished PhD dissertation. Institute Education, University of London.
Bryan, B.(1999). Some correspondences between West African and Jamaican Creole Speakers in Learning Standard English. In L. Carrington, P. Christie, B. Lalla and V. Pollard (Eds.), *Studies in Caribbean Language II.* UWI St Augustine: School of Education.
Bryan, B. (2001). The role of linguistic markers in manufacturing consent: Jamaican Creole in the classroom. *In Respect Due: Papers on Caribbean English and Creole, in honor of*

Professor Robert Le Page, a Pioneer (pp.79–96). Mona, Kingston: The University of the West Indies Press.

Bryan, B. (2004). Reconciling contradictions and moving for change: Towards a Language Education Policy for Jamaica. In Transforming the Educational Landscape through Curriculum Change. UWI, Mona: Institute of Education.

Bryne, D. (2001) *Understanding the Urban*. London: Palgrave.

Bullock Report (1975). *A Language for Life*. London. HMSO.

Byron, M. (1994) Post-war Caribbean Migration to Britain. The Unfinished Cycle. Aldershot: Avebury.

Campbell-Stephens, R. (2011) What Free Schools Might Offer: Reflections by Black Parents and Educators. *Race Equality Teaching* 29 (2): 34–37.

Carrington, L.D. (2001). The status of Creole in the Caribbean. In P. Christie (Ed.), *Due Respect: Papers on English and English-Related Creoles in the Caribbean in Honor of Professor Robert Le Page* (pp. 24–36). Mona, Kingston: University of the West Indies Press.

Carrington, L. D. and Borely, C. (1977). *The Language Arts Syllabus 1975: Comment and Countercomment*. St. Augustine, Trinidad: University of the West Indies.

Cassen, R. & Kingdon, G. (2007) *Tackling Low Educational Achievement*. York: Joseph Rowntree Foundation.

Caws, Peter (1997). *Structuralism: A Philosophy for the Human Sciences*. New York: Humanity Books.

Chanda-Goo, S. (2006) *South Asian Communities; Catalysts for Educational Change*. Stoke-on-Trent: Trentham.

Chase-Dunn, Christopher and Peter Grimes (1995). "World-Systems Analysis." *Annual Review of Sociology*, 21, 387–417.

Chase-Dunn, Christopher and Richard Rubinson (1977). "Toward a Structural Perspective on the World-System." *Politics & Society*, 7: 4, 453–476.

Chase-Dunn, Christopher (1975). "The effects of international economic dependence on development and inequality: A cross-national study." *American Sociological Review*, 40, 720–738.

Chiswick, B. (1978) The effect of Americanization on the Earnings of Foreign Born Men. *Journal of Political Economy*, 86 (5), pp. 897–922.

Christie, P. (1982). 'Trends in Jamaican English: Increasing deviance or emerging standards.' Paper presented at the biennial conference of the Society for Caribbean Linguistics, Suriname.

Christie, P. (Ed.). (2001). *Due Respect: Papers on English and English-Related Creoles in the Caribbean in Honor of Professor Robert Le Page*. Mona, Kingston: University of the West Indies Press.

Christie, P. (2003). *Language in Jamaica*. Kingston, Jamaica: Arawak.

Clark, K and Drinkwater, S. (2007) *Ethnic Minorities in the Labor Market: Dynamics and Diversity*. Abingdon: Joseph Rowntree Foundation. Policy Press.

Clark, Robert P. (1997). *The Global Imperative: An Interpretive History of the Spread of Humankind*. Boulder, Colorado: Westview Press.

Clarke, John Henrik, et. al. (eds.) (1970). *Black Titan: W.E.B. Du Bois*. Boston: Beacon Press.

Clark, P. (1988) *Prejudice and Your Child*. Middletown, Connecticut: Wesleyan University Press.

Coard, B. (1971) *How the Education West Indian Child is Made Educationally Subnormal in the British School System: The Scandal of the Black Child in School*. London: New Beacon Books.

Cohen, J. (2002). *Protestantism and Capitalism: The Mechanisms of Influence*. New York: Aldine de Gruyter.

Cole, M. (2011) Racism and Education in the UK and US. Palgrave Macmillan. New York.

Collins, C., Kenway, J. and McLeod, J. (2000). *Factors influencing the educational performance of males and females in schools and their initial destinations after leaving school*. Geelong: Deakin University.

Collinson, Diane (1987). *Fifty Major Philosophers: A Reference Guide*. London: Routledge.

Commonwealth Immigrants Advisory Council (CIAC) (1964) Second Report, Cmnd 2266. London: HMSO.

Corrodus, A. (1987). Error Consistency in the Writing of Students in a Jamaican Secondary School. Unpublished MA thesis, Faculty of Education, UWI, Mona.

Coser, Lewis (1956). *The functions of social conflict.* New York: The Free Press.

Covino, William A. and David A. Jolliffe (1995). *Rhetoric: concepts, definitions, boundaries.* Needham Heights, Massachusetts: Allyn and Bacon.

Cox, C.B. and Boyson, R. (1977) *Black Paper 1977.* London: Temple-Smith.

Craig, D.R. (1976). Bidialectal education: Creole and Standard in the West Indies. *IJSL* 8: 93–134 (2001). Language Education Revisited in the Commonwealth Caribbean. In P. Christie (Ed.) *Due Respect. Papers on English and English-related Creoles in the Caribbean in Honor of Professor Robert Le Page* (pp.61–78). Mona, Kingston: University of the West Indies Press.

Crothers, Charles (2003). "Technical Advances in General Sociological Theory: The Potential Contribution of Post-Structurationist Sociology." *Perspectives*, 26: (3), 3–6.

Crouch, Stanley (1993). "Who are We? Where Did We Come From? Where Are We Going?" In Gerald Early (Ed.), *Lure and Loathing: Essays on Race, Identity, and the Ambivalence of Assimilation* (pp. 80–94). New York: The Penguin Press.

Culler, Jonathan (1976). *Saussure.* Great Britain: Fontana/Collins.

Curtin, Philip D. (1969). *The Atlantic Slave Trade: A Census.* Madison, Wisconsin: The University of Wisconsin Press.

Dahrendorf, Ralf (1959). *Class and Class Conflict in Industrial Society.* Stanford, California: Stanford University Press.

DeCamp, D. (1971). The study of Pidgin and Creole Languages (pp. 13–43). In D. Hymes (Ed.) *Pidginization and Creolization of Languages.* Cambridge: Cambridge University DES (1965) The Education of Immigrants. Circular 7/65. London: DES.

Degler, Carl N. (1972). "Slavery and the Genesis of American Race Prejudice." In Donald Noel (Ed.), *The Origins of American Slavery and Racism* (pp. 59–80). Ohio: Charles E. Merrill Publishing Co.

DeMarco, Joseph P. (1983). *The Social Thought of W.E.B. Du Bois.* Lanham, MD: University Press of America.

Demie, F. (2005) Achievement of Black Caribbean Pupils in British Schools: Good Practice in Lambeth Schools. *British Educational Research Journal.* 3 (4): pp. 481–508.

Demireva, N. (2009) *Ethnicity and Social Organization: Changes and Challenges.* website: www.beyondcurrenthorizons.org.uk.

Devonish, H. (1986). *Language and Liberation: Creole Language Politics in the Caribbean.* London: Karia Press.

Department for Children, Schools and Families (2007) Statistical First Release National Curriculum Assessment, GCSE and Equivalent Attainment and Post-16 Attainment by Pupil Characteristics, in England, (2007). http://dcsf.gov.uk/rsgateway/DB/SFR. Accessed on Friday July 18, 2008.

Department for Community and Local Government (2012) *Creating the Conditions for Integration* http://www.communities.gov.uk/documents/communities/pdf/2092103.pdf. Accessed on Monday May 5 2012.

Department for Education (2010) *The Importance of Teaching the Schools White paper 2010.* London: Department for Education.

Department for Education (2012) Statistical First Release, GCSE and Equivalent Attainment by Pupil Characteristics in England, 2010/11. http://www.education.gov.uk/rsgateway/DB/SFR/s000977/index.shtml. Accessed on Tuesday January 10, 2012.

Department for Education and Skills (2003) *Aiming High: Raising the Achievement of Minority Ethnic Pupils.* Consultation Document. London: Department for Education and Skills.

Department for Education and Skills (2004) Five Year Strategy for Children and Learners. https://www.education.gov.uk/publications/standard/publicationdetail/page1/DFES-03902-2006. Accessed on Thursday April 24, 2012.

Department for Education and Skills ((2006) *Ethnicity and Education: The Evidence on Minority Ethnic Pupils Aged 15–16*. Research Topic Papers. London: Department for Education and Skills.

Diop, Cheikh A. (1981). *Civilization or Barbarism: An Authentic Anthropology*. New York: Lawrence Hill Books.

Dogson, E. (1986) *Motherland: West Indian Women to Britain in the 1950s*. London: Heinemann Education Books.

Douglas, M. (1986). *How Institutions Think*. New York: Syracuse University Press.

Drake, St. Claire (1965). "The Social and Economic Status of the Negro in the United States." In Talcott Parsons and Kenneth B. Clark (Eds.), *The Negro American* (pp. 3–46). Boston: Houghton Mifflin Company.

Drew, D. and Gray, J. (1990) The Fifth-Year Examination Achievement of Black Young People in England and Wales. *Educational Research* 32 (2): 107–117.

Driver, G. (1980) How West Indians do Better at School (especially the girls) *New Society* January 17: pp.11–114.

Du Bois, W.E.B. (1995 [1903]). *The Souls of Black Folk*. New York: Penguin Putnam Inc.

Du Bois, W.E.B. (1984 [1940]). *Dusk of Dawn: An Essay toward an Autobiography of a Race Concept*. New Brunswick and London: Transaction Books.

Du Bois, W.E.B. (1971a [1897]). "The Conservation of Races." In Julius Lester (Ed.), *The Seventh Son: The Thought and Writings of W.E.B. Du Bois* (Volume I) (pp. 176–187). New York: Random House.

Du Bois, W.E.B. (1971b [1935]). "A Negro Nation Within The Nation." In Julius Lester (Ed.), *The Seventh Son: The Thought and Writings of W.E.B. Du Bois* (Volume II) (pp. 399–407). New York: Random House.

Du Bois, W.E.B. (1970 [1939]). *Black Folk, Then and Now: An Essay in the History and Sociology of the Negro Race*. New York: Octagon Books.

Du Bois, W. E. B. (1968). *The Autobiography of W.E.B. Du Bois: A Soliloquy on Viewing My Life from the Last Decade of its First Century*. US: International Publishers Co., Inc.

Du Bois, W.E.B. (1967 [1899]). *The Philadelphia Negro: A Social Study*. New York: Schocken Books.

Durkheim, Emile (1984 [1893]). *The Division of Labor in Society* (W.D. Halls, Trans.). New York: The Free Press.

Dustmann, C. and Fabbri, F. (2000) *Language Proficiency and Labor Market Performance of Immigrants in the UK*. Discussion Paper No 156, IZA Bonn.

Eagleton, Terry (1999). *Marx*. New York: Routledge.

Eagleton, Terry (1991). *Ideology: An Introduction*. London: Verso.

Early, Gerald (ed.) (1993). *Lure and Loathing: Essays on Race, Identity , and the Ambivalence of Assimilation*. New York: The Penguin Press.

Edgar, Andrew and Peter Sedgwick (Eds.) (1999). *Key Concepts in Cultural Theory*. London: Routledge.

Education and Skills Select Committee. Minutes of Evidence to the House of Common: May 7, 2003. http://www.publications.parliament.uk/pa/cm200203/cmselect/cmeduski/513/305070. Accessed on Thursday February 21 2008.

Edwards, V. (1979). *The West Indian Language Issue in British Schools: Challenges and Responses*. London: Routledge and Paul.

Edwards, V. (1986). *Language in a Black Community*: Clevedon, Avon: Multilingual Matters. Economic and Social Survey (2001). Jamaica: Planning Institute of Jamaica.

Elkins, Stanley (1959). *Slavery: A Problem in American Institutional and Intellectual Life*. Chicago: University of Chicago Press.

Elkins, Stanley M. (1972). "The Dynamics of Unopposed Capitalism." In Donald Noel (Ed.), *The Origins of American Slavery and Racism* (pp. 45–58). Ohio: Charles E. Merrill Publishing Co.

Engels, Frederick (2000 [1884]. *The Origin of the Family, Private Property, and the State*. New York: Pathfinder Press.

Eysenck, H.J. (1971) *Race, Intelligence and Education*. London: Temple-Smith.

Foster, M. (1991). Constancy, Connectedness and Constraints in the lives of African. American Teachers. *NWSA Journal* 3 (2): 233–261.

Fox, C. (1993). *At the very edge of the forest: The influence of literature on storytelling by children*. London: Cassell.

Fanon, Frantz (1967). *Black Skin, White Masks* (Charles Lam Markmann, Trans.). New York: Grove Press.

Fanon, Frantz (1963). *The Wretched of the Earth* (Constance Farrington, Trans). New York: Grove Press.

Fogel, Robert W. (2003). *The Slavery Debates, 1952–1990: A Retrospective*. Baton Rouge: Louisiana State University Press.

Foner, Eric (1988). *Reconstruction: America's Unfinished Revolution 1863 –1877.* New York: Harper & Row Publishers. .

Foner, Eric (1990). *A Short History of Reconstruction 1863 –1877.* New York: Harper & Row Publishers .

Foner, P. (1979) *Jamaica Farewell.* Jamaican Migrants in London: London: Routledge Kegan & Paul.

Fordham, S. & Ogbu, J. (1986) Black Student' School Success: Coping with the Burden of Acting White. *The Urban Review*. 18 (3): 176–206.

Foucault, Michel (1977). *Discipline and Punish: The Birth of the Prison* (Alan Sheridan, Trans.). London: Penguin Books.

Franklin, John Hope and Alfred A. Moss Jr. (2000). *From Slavery to Freedom: A History of African Americans* (Eighth Edition). New York: Alfred A. Knopf.

Fraser, Nancy (1997). *Justice Interruptus: Critical Reflections on the "Postsocialist" Condition*. New York & London: Routledge.

Frazier, Franklin E. (1939). *The Negro Family in America*. Chicago: University of Chicago Press.

Frazier, Franklin E. (1957). *Black Bourgeoisie: The Rise of a New Middle Class*. New York: The Free Press.

Frazier, Franklin E. (1968). *The Free Negro Family*. New York: Arno Press and The New York Times.

Freud, Sigmund (1989 [1940]. *An Outline of Psycho-Analysis* (James Strachey, Trans. and Editor). New York: W.W. Norton & Company.

Freud, Sigmund (1989 [1921]. *Group Psychology and the Analysis of the Ego* (James Strachey, Trans. and Editor). New York: W.W. Norton & Company.

Freud, Sigmund (1989 [1917]. *Introductory Lectures on Psycho-Analysis* (James Strachey, Trans. and Editor). New York: W.W. Norton & Company.

Fryer, P. (1984) Staying Power: The History of Black People in Britain. London: Pluto Press.

Gadamer, Hans-Georg (2002). *Truth and Method* (Second, Revised Edition, Joel Weinsheimer and Donald G. Marshall, Trans.). New York: Continuum.

Gaine, C. and George, R. (1999). *Gender, Race, and Class in Schooling. A New Introduction*. London: Falmer Press.

Gartman, David (2002). "Bourdieu's Theory of Cultural Change: Explication, Application, Critique." *Sociological Theory* 20 (2): 255–277.

Gates, Henry L. et al. (Eds.) (1997). *The Norton Anthology: African American Literature* . New York: W.W. Norton & Company Inc.

Gates, Henry Louis, Jr. and Cornel West (1996). *The Future of the Race*. New York: Vintage Books.

Gillborn, D. (2001) 'Racism, Policy and the (mis) education of Black Children' in R. Majors (Ed). *Educating Our Black Children* (pp 13–27). London. Routledge Falmer.

Gillborn, D. (2008) *Racism and Education: Coincidence or Conspiracy.* London: Routledge Falmer.

Gillborn, D. and Gipps, C. (1996) *Recent Research into the Achievements of Ethnic Minority Pupils*. London: Ofsted.

Gillborn, D. and Mirza, H.S. (2000) *Educational Inequality. Mapping Race, Class and Gender*. London: Ofsted.

Gilroy, P. (1990) 'The end of Anti-Racism.' *New Community*. 17 (1): pp. 71–83.

94   *References Cited*

Geertz, Clifford (1973). *The Interpretation of Cultures*. New York: Basic Books.
Geertz, Clifford (2000). *Local Knowledge: Further Essays in Interpretive Anthropology*. New York: Basic Books.
Genovese, Eugene (1974). *Roll, Jordan, Roll*. New York: Pantheon Books.
Geronimus, Arline T. and F. Phillip Thompson. "To Denigrate, Ignore, or Disrupt: Racial Inequality in Health and the Impact of a Policy-induced Breakdown of African American Communities." *Du Bois Review* 1; 2: 247–279.
Giddens, Anthony (1984). *The Constitution of Society: Outline of the Theory of Structuration*. Cambridge: Polity Press.
Gilroy, Paul (1987) *There Ain't no Blacks in the Union Jack: The Cultural Politics of Race and Nation*. London: Routledge.
Gilroy, Paul (1993). *The Black Atlantic: Modernity and Double Consciousness*. Cambridge, Massachusetts: Harvard.
Glazer, Nathan and Daniel P. Moynihan (1963). *Beyond the Melting Pot*. Cambridge: Harvard University Press.
Gooding-Williams, Robert (1996). "Outlaw, Appiah, and Du Bois's 'The Conservation of Races.'" In Bell W. Bernard et al. (Eds.), *W.E.B. Du Bois on Race and Culture: Philosophy, Politics, and Poetics* (pp. 39–56). New York and London: Routledge.
Gramsci, Antonio (1959). *The Modern Prince, and Other Writings*. New York: International Publishers.
Greene, M. & Way, N. (2005) Self-Esteem Trajectories among Ethnic Minority Adolescents: A Growth Curve Analysis of the Patterns and Predictors of Change. *Journal of Research on Adolescence*, (15), 151–178.
Grutter v. Bollinger et al, 539 U.S. 02-241 (2003); 13 (Slip Opinion).
Gutiérrez, Ramón A. (2004). "Internal Colonialism: An American Theory of Race." *Du Bois Review*, 1; 2: 281–295.
Gutman, Herbert (1976). *The Black Family in Slavery and Freedom 1750–1925*. New York: Pantheon Books.
Habermas, Jürgen (1987). *The Theory of Communicative Action: Lifeworld and System: A Critique of Functionalist Reason* (Volume 2, Thomas McCarthy, Trans.). Boston: Beacon Press.
Habermas, Jürgen (1984). *The Theory of Communicative Action: Reason and the Rationalization of Society* (Volume 1, Thomas McCarthy, Trans.). Boston: Beacon Press.
Handlin, Oscar and Mary F. Handlin (1972). "The Origins of Negro Slavery." In Donald Noel (Ed.), *The Origins of American Slavery and Racism* (pp. 21–44). Ohio: Charles E. Merrill Publishing Co.
Harding, Vincent (1981). *There is a River: The Black Struggle for Freedom in America*. New York: Harcourt Brace & Company.
Hare, Nathan (1991). *The Black Anglo-Saxons*. Chicago: Third World Press.
Harris, Marvin. (1999). *Theories of culture in postmodern times*. Walnut Creek, California: AltaMira Press.
Harris, David R. and Jeremiah Joseph Sim (2002). "Who is Multiracial? Assessing the Complexity of Lived Race." *American Sociological Review* 67; 4: 614–627.
Heath, A. and Cheung, S. (2006) *Ethnic Penalties in the Labor Market: Employers and Discrimination*. Research report No 341. London: Department of Work and Pensions.
Heath, A. and Yu, S. (2005) *Explaining Ethnic Minority Disadvantage* (pp.187–224). In: Heath, A., Ermisch, J. and Gallie, D. *Understanding social change*. Oxford, Oxford University Press.
Hegel, G.W.F. (1977 [1807]). *Phenomenology of Spirit* (A.V. Miller, Trans.). Oxford: Oxford University Press.
Heidegger, Martin (1962 [1927]). *Being and Time*. New York: HarperSanFrancisco.
Helle, H.J. and S.N. Eisenstadt (ed.) (1985). *Macro-Sociological Theory: Perspectives on Sociological Theory* (Volume 1). United Kingdom: J.W. Arrowsmith Ltd.
Helle, H.J. and S.N. Eisenstadt (ed.) (1985). *Micro-Sociological Theory: Perspectives on Sociological Theory* (Volume 2). United Kingdom: J.W. Arrowsmith Ltd.

Herrnstein, R. and Murray, C. (1994) *The Bell Curve: Intelligence and Class Structure in American Life*. New York: The Free Press.

Herskovits, Melville J. (1958 [1941]). *The Myth of the Negro Past*. Boston: Beacon Press.

Hewitt, R. (1986) *White Talk Black Talk: Inter-Racial Friendship and Communication amongst Adolescents*. Cambridge: Cambridge University Press.

Hiro, D. (1973*) Black British, White British*. Harmondsworth: Penguin.

HMSO (1991) *Aspects of Britain's Ethnic Minorities*. London: H.M.S.O.

Hochschild, Jennifer L. (1984). *The New American Dilemma: Liberal Democracy and School Desegregation*. New Haven: Yale University Press.

Hogue, Lawrence W. (1996). *Race, Modernity, Postmodernity: A look at the History and the Literatures of People of Color Since the 1960s*. Albany: State University of New York Press.

Holloway, Joseph E. (ed.) (1990a). *Africanisms in American Culture*. Bloomington and Indianapolis: Indiana University Press.

Holloway, Joseph E. (1990b). "The Origins of African-American Culture." In Joseph Holloway (Ed.), *Africanisms in American Culture* (19–33). Bloomington and Indianapolis: Indiana University Press.

Holm, J. (1988). *Pidgins and Creoles*. Cambridge: Cambridge University Press.

Holt, Thomas (1990). "The Political Uses of Alienation: W.E.B. Du Bois on Politics, Race, and Culture, 1903–1940." *American Quarterly* 42 (2): 301–323.

Horkheimer, Max and Theodor W. Adorno (2000 [1944]. *Dialectic of Enlightenment* (John Cumming, Trans.). New York: Continuum.

Horne, Gerald (1986). *Black and Red: W.E.B. Du Bois and the Afro-American Response to the Cold War, 1944–1963*. New York: State University of New York Press.

House, James S. (1977). "The Three Faces of Social Psychology." *Sociometry* 40: 161–177.

House, James S. (1981). "Social Structure and Personality." In Morris Rosenberg and Ralph Turner (Eds.), *Sociological Perspectives on Social Psychology* (pp. 525–561). New York: Basic Books.

Hudson, Kenneth and Andrea Coukos (2005). "The Dark Side of the Protestant Ethic: A Comparative Analysis of Welfare Reform." *Sociological Theory* 23 (1): 1–24.

Hunt, C. (2004) Inequality, Achievement and African-Caribbean Pupils. *Race Equality Teaching*: 22 (3) 31–36.

Hunton, Alphaeus w. (1970). "W.E.B. Du Bois: the meaning of his life." In John Henrik Clarke et al (Eds.), *Black Titan: W.E.B. Du Bois* (pp. 131–137). Boston: Beacon Press.

Inkeles, Alex (1959). "Personality and Social Structure." In Robert K. Merton, Leonard Broom, and Leonard S. Cottrell, Jr. (eds.), *Sociology Today* (pp. 249–276). New York: Basic Books.

Inkeles, Alex (1960). "Industrial man: The Relation of Status, Experience, and Value." *American Journal of Sociology* 66: 1–31.

Inkeles, Alex (1969). "Making Men Modern: On the causes and consequences of individual change in six developing countries." *American Journal of Sociology* 75: 208–225.

James, C.L.R., Breitman, G. & Keemer, E. (1980) Fighting Racism in World War 1. New York: Monad Press.

Jameson, Fredric and Masao Miyoshi (ed.). (1998). *The Cultures of Globalization*. Durham: Duke University Press.

Jensen, A. (1969) 'How much can we boost IQ and Scholastic Ability?' *Harvard Educational Review* Vol 39: 1–23.

Johns, L. (2011) Will we ever have a Black Prime Minister? *The Telegraph* http://www.telegraph.co.uk/news/politics/8590456/Will-we-ever-have-a-black-prime-minister.html. Accessed on June 23, 2011.

Jones, G.S. (1971). *Outcast London: A Study in the Relationship Between Classes in Victorian Society*. Oxford: Clarendon Press.

Jordan, Winthrop D. (1972). "Modern Tensions and the Origins of American Slavery." In Donald Noel (Ed.), *The Origins of American Slavery and Racism* (pp. 81–94). Ohio: Charles E. Merrill Publishing Co.

Kardiner, Abram and Lionel Ovesey (1962 [1951]. *The Mark of Oppression: Explorations in the Personality of the American Negro*. Meridian Ed.

Karenga, Maulana (1993). *Introduction to Black Studies*. California: The University of Sankore Press.

Kellner, Douglas (2002). "Theorizing Globalization." *Sociological Theory*, 20: (3), 285–305.

Kneller, George F. (1964). *Introduction to the Philosophy of Education*. New York: John Wiley & Sons, Inc.

Kogan, M. (1975) *Dispersal in the Ealing School System*. Report to the Race Relation Board. July London: RRB.

Kuhn, Thomas S. (1996). *The Structure of Scientific Revolutions* (Third Edition). Chicago: The University of Chicago Press.

Labov, W. (1973). The Logic of nonstandard English. In P.N. Keddie (Ed.), *Tinker, Tailor: The Myth of Cultural Deprivation* (pp 21–66). Harmondsworth: Penguin.

Laclau, Ernesto and Chantal Mouffe (1985). *Hegemony & Socialist Strategy: Towards a Radical Democratic Politics*. New York and London: Verso.

Layton-Henry, Z. (1984) *The Politics of Race in Britain*. London: Allen & Unwin.

Lester, Julius (ed.) (1971). *The Seventh Son: The Thought and Writings of W.E.B. Du Bois* (Volume I). New York: Random House.

Lester, Julius (ed.) (1971). *The Seventh Son: The Thought and Writings of W.E.B. Du Bois* (Volume II). New York: Random House.

Lewis, David Levering (1993). *W.E.B. Du Bois: Biography of a Race 1868–1919*. New York: Henry Holt and Company.

Levine, Lawrence W. (1977). *Black Culture and Black Consciousness: Afro-American Folk Thought from Slavery to Freedom*. New York: Oxford University Press.

Lévi-Strauss, Claude (1963). *Structural Anthropology* (Claire Jacobson and Brooke Schoepf, Trans.). New York: Basic Books.

Lincoln, Eric C. and Lawrence H. Mamiya (1990). *The Black Church in the African American Experience*. Durham and London: Duke University Press.

Lowenthal, D. (1972) *West Indian Societies*. Oxford: Oxford University Press.

Luckmann, Thomas (Ed.) (1978). *Phenomenology and Sociology: Selected Readings*. New York: Penguin Books.

Lukács, Georg (1971). *History and Class Consciousness: Studies in Marxist Dialectics* (Rodney Livingstone, Trans.). Cambridge, Massachusetts: The MIT Press.

Lukács, Georg (2000). *A Defence of History and Class Consciousness: Tailism and the Dialectic* (Esther Leslie, Trans.). London and New York: Verso.

Luscombe, David (1997). *A History of Western Philosophy: Medieval Thought*. Oxford: Oxford University Press.

Lyman, Stanford M. (1997). *Postmodernism and a Sociology of the Absurd and Other Essays on the "Nouvelle Vague" in American Social Science*. Fayetteville: The University of Arkansas Press.

Lyman, Stanford M. and Arthur J. Vidich (1985). *American Sociology: Worldly Rejections of Religion and Their Directions*. New Haven and London: Yale University Press.

Lyman, Stanford M. (1972). *The Black American in Sociological Thought*. New York.

Machan Ghaill, M. (1994) *The Making Men, Masculinities, Sexualities and Schooling*. Buckingham: Open University Press.

Machin, S. and McNally, S. (2005). Gender and Student Achievement in English Schools. *Oxford Review of Economic Policy* 21(3): 357–372.

Mageo, Jeannette Marie (1998). *Theorizing Self in Samoa: Emotions, Genders, and Sexualities*. Ann Arbor: The University of Michigan Press.

Maguire, M. Wooldridge, T. & Pratt-Adams, S. (2006) *The Urban Primary School*. Maidenhead, Berks: Open University Press.

Massey, D.S., and Denton, N.A. (1993). *American Apartheid: Segregation and the Making of the Underclass*. Cambridge, MA: Harvard University Press.

Marable, Manning (1986). *W.E.B. Du Bois: Black Radical Democrat*. Boston: Twayne Publishers.

Marcuse, Herbert (1964). *One-Dimensional Man*. Boston: Beacon Press.

Marcuse, Herbert (1974). *Eros and Civilization: A Philosophical Inquiry into Freud*. Boston: Beacon Press.

Marshall, Gordon (Ed.) (1998). *A Dictionary of Sociology* (Second edition). Oxford: Oxford University Press.

Martin, R. and Rowthorn, R, (Eds.) (1986) The Geography of Deindustrialization, London: Macmillan.

Matheson, M. and Matheson, D. (2000). Language of Scotland: Culture and the classroom. *Comparative Education* 36 (2): 211–221.

Maugham, B. and Rutter, M (1986) Black Pupils Progress in Secondary School—II Examination Attainment. *British Journal of Development Psychology* 4: 19–23.

Marx, Karl and Friedrich Engels (1964). *The Communist Manifesto*. London, England: Penguin Books.

Marx, Karl (1992 [1867]). *Capital: A Critique of Political Economy* (Volume 1, Samuel Moore and Edward Aveling, Trans.). New York: International Publishers.

Marx, Karl (1998 [1845]). *The German Ideology*. New York: Prometheus Books.

Mason, Patrick L. (1996). "Race, Culture, and the Market." *Journal of Black Studies*, 26: 6, 782–808.

McIntosh, N. and Smith, D. (1974) *The Extent of Racial Discrimination, Political and Economic Planning Broadsheet*. No 547, London, Political and Economic Planning.

McIntyre, W.D. (2001) *A Guide to the Contemporary Commonwealth*. Palgrave.

Mead, George Herbert (1978 [1910]). "What Social Objects Must Psychology Presuppose." In Thomas Luckmann (Ed.), *Phenomenology and Sociology: Selected Readings* (17–24). New York: Penguin Books.

Macpherson, W. (1999) *The Stephen Lawrence Inquiry*. CM4262.I. London: The Stationery Office.

Meier, August (1963). *Negro Thought in America, 1880–1915: Racial Ideologies in the Age of Booker T. Washington*. Ann Arbor: The University of Michigan Press.

Meier, August and Elliott M. Rudwick (1976 [1966]). *From Plantation to Ghetto; an Interpretive History of American Negroes*. New York: Hill and Wang.

Miller, E. (1990). *Jamaican Society and High Schooling*. University of the West Indies, Mona: Institute of Social and Economic Research.

Milner, D. (1975) *Children and Race*. Harmondsworth: Penguin.

Ministry of Education and Culture (2000). *The Education System: Jamaica*. University of the West Indies, School of Education Documentation Centre.

Mirza, H. (2005) The more things change, the more they stay the same: Assessing Black Underachievement 35 years on. In B Richardson. (Ed.) *Tell it like it is. How our School fail Black Children* (pp.111–119). Stoke-on-Trent: Trentham Books.

Mitton, L. and Aspinall (2011) *Black Africans in the UK: Integration or Segregation*. UPTAP Research Findings January 2011 http://www.uptap.net/wordpress/wp-content/uploads/2011/01/uptap-findings-mitton-jan-11.pdf. Accessed on Monday January 9, 2012.

Mocombe, Paul C. (2004). "Who Makes Race Matter in Post-Industrial Capitalist America?" *Race, Gender & Class* 11, 4: 30–47.

Mocombe, Paul C. and Tomlin, C. (2010) *The Oppositional Culture Theory*. Lanham: M.D. University Press of America.

Mocombe, Paul C., Carol Tomlin, and Cecile Wright (2014). "A Racial Caste in Class: Race and Class Distinctions within Black Communities in the United States and United Kingdom." *Race, Gender, & Class*, 21, 3-4: 101-121.

Mocombe, Paul C., Carol Tomlin, Cecile Wright (2014). *Race and Class Distinctions Within Black Communities: A Racial Caste in Class*. Routledge Research in Race and Ethnicity (Vol. 9). New York and London: Routledge.

Mocombe, Paul C., Carol Tomlin, and Cecile Wright (2014). "A Structural Approach to Understanding Black British Caribbean Academic Underachievement in the United Kingdom." *Journal of Social Science for Policy Implications*, 2, 2: 37-58.

Mocombe, Paul C., Carol Tomlin, and Victoria Showunmi (2014). "Jesus and the Streets: A Hermeneutical Framework for Understanding the Intraracial Gender Academic Achievement Gap in Black Urban America and the United Kingdom." *Language and Sociocultural Theory*, 1, 2: 125-152.

Mocombe, Paul C. and Carol Tomlin (2013). *Language, Literacy, and Pedagogy in Postindustrial Societies: The Case of Black Academic Underachievement*. Routledge Research in Education (Vol. 97). New York and London: Routledge.

Mocombe, Paul C., Carol Tomlin, and Cecile Wright (2013). "Karl Marx, Ludwig Wittgenstein, and Black Underachievement in the United States and United Kingdom." *Diaspora, Indigenous, and Minority Education*, 7, 4: 214-228.

Mocombe, Paul C., Carol Tomlin, and Cecile Wright (2013). "Postindustrial Capitalism, Social Class Language Games, and Black Underachievement in the United States and United Kingdom." *Mind, Culture, and Activity*, 20, 4: 358-371.

Mocombe, Paul C. (2012). *Liberal Bourgeois Protestantism: The Metaphysics of Globalization*. Studies in Critical Social Sciences (Vol. 41). Leiden, Netherlands: Brill Publications.

Mocombe, Paul (2011). "Role Conflict and Black Underachievement." *The Journal for Critical Education Policy Studies*, 9, 2: 165-185.

Mocombe, Paul (2011). "A Social Structural Reinterpretation of 'the Burden of Acting White': A Hermeneutical Analysis." *Discourse: Studies in the Cultural Politics of Education*, 32, 1: 85-97.

Mocombe, Paul C. and Carol Tomlin (2010). *Oppositional Culture Theory*. Maryland: University Press of America.

Mocombe, Paul (2010). "Why Haiti is Maligned in the Western World: The Contemporary Significance of Bois Caiman and the Haitian Revolution." *Encuentros*, 8, 16: 31-43.

Mocombe, Paul C. (2009). *The Liberal Black Protestant Heterosexual Bourgeois Male: From W.E.B. Du Bois to Barack Obama*. Maryland: University Press of America.

Mocombe, Paul C. (2008). *The Soulless Souls of Black Folk: A Sociological Reconsideration of Black Consciousness as Du Boisian Double Consciousness*. Maryland: University Press of America.

Mocombe, Paul C. (2007). *Education in Globalization*. Maryland: University Press of America.

Mocombe, Paul (2006). "The Sociolinguistic Nature of Black Academic Failure in Capitalist Education: A Reevaluation of 'Language in the Inner City' and its Social Function, Acting White'." *Race, Ethnicity and Education*, 9, 4: 395-407.

Mocombe, Paul (2006). "The Gentrification of Africa in the Contemporary Capitalist World System: Reply to Kelsall and Gberie." *Globalizations*, 3, 3: 413-417.

Mocombe, Paul (2005). "Where Did Freire Go Wrong? Pedagogy in Globalization: The Grenadian Example." *Race, Gender & Class*, 12, 2: 178-199.

Mocombe, Paul (2004). "Who Makes Race Matter in Post-Industrial Capitalist America?" *Race, Gender & Class*, 11, 4: 30-47.

Mocombe, Paul (2003). "Rhetorical "Being": Understanding Agency in Structur(ealism)." *FACS*, 6: 155-164.

Model, S. and Fisher, G. (2002) Unions between Blacks and Whites: England and the US Compared. *Ethnic and Racial Studies* 25 (5) pp 728–754.

Modood, T., Berthoud, R., Lakey, J., Nazroo, J., Smith, P., Virdee, S. and Beishon, S. (1997) *Ethnic Minorities in Britain: Diversity and Disadvantage*. Policy Studies Institute, London.

Moore, Jerry D. (1997). *Visions of Culture: An Introduction to Anthropological Theories and Theorists*. Walnut Creek, California: AltaMira Press.

Mortimore, P (2007) 'Will Academies take the easy options.' *Education Guardian*, Tuesday, November 6, p. 4.

Moynihan, Daniel P. (1965). *The Negro Family*. Washington, D.C.: Office of Planning and Research, US Department of Labor.

Mullard, C. (1982) 'Multiracial Education in Britain: from Assimilation to Cultural Pluralism' in J. (Ed.) (1982) Race, Migration and Schooling.pp.120–33. London: Holt, Rinehart and Winston.

Murray, Charles (1984). *Losing Ground: American Social Policy 1950–1980*. New York: Basic Books.

Murray, R.N. & Gbedemah, G.L (1983) *Foundations of Education in the Caribbean*. London: Hodder & Stoughton.

Myrdal, Gunnar (1944). *An American Dilemma: The Negro Problem and Modern Democracy*. New York: Harper & Row Publishers.

Nash, Gary B. (1972). "Red, White and Black: The Origins of Racism in Colonial America." In Donald Noel (Ed.), *The Origins of American Slavery and Racism* (pp. 131–152). Ohio: Charles E. Merrill Publishing Co.

Nietzsche, Friedrich (1956). *The Birth of Tragedy* and *The Genealogy of Morals* (Francis Golffing, Trans.). New York: Anchor Books.

Nobles, Wade (1987). *African American Families: Issues, Ideas, and Insights*. Oakland: Black Family Institute.

Noel, Donald L. (Ed.) (1972). *The Origins of American Slavery and Racism*. Columbus, Ohio: Charles E. Merrill Publishing Co.

Noel, Donald L. (1972). "A Theory of the Origins of Ethnic Stratification." In Donald Noel (Ed.), *The Origins of American Slavery and Racism* (pp. 106–127). Ohio: Charles E. Merrill Publishing Co.

Noel, Donald L. (1972). "Slavery and the Rise of Racism." In Donald Noel (Ed.), *The Origins of American Slavery and Racism* (pp. 153–174). Ohio: Charles E. Merrill Publishing Co.

Obeyesekere, Gananath (1997 [1992]). *The Apotheosis of Captain Cook: European Mythmaking in the Pacific*. Hawaii: Bishop Museum Press.

Office for National Statistics: Statistical Bulletin (2011) Population Estimates by Ethnic Group 2002–2009. http://www.ons.gov.uk/ons/taxonomy/index.html?nscl=Population+Estimates+by+Ethnic+Group Accessed on Wednesday January 4, 2012.

Ogbu, J. (1992) Understanding Cultural Diversity and Learning. *Educational Researcher* November (21): 5–14.

O'Leary N. C., Murphy, P.D., Drinkwater S.J. and Blackaby D.H. (2001). `English Language Fluency and the Ethnic Wage Gap for Men in England and Wales', *Economic Issues* (6): 21–32.

Ortner, Sherry (1984). "Theory in Anthropology Since the Sixties," *Comparative Studies in Society and History* 26: 126–66.

Outlaw, Lucius (1996). "Conserve" Races?: In Defense of W.E.B. Du Bois." In Bernard W. Bell et al (Eds.), *W.E.B. Du Bois on Race and Culture: Philosophy, Politics, and Poetics* (pp. 15–38). New York and London: Routledge.

Parsons, Talcott (1951). *The Social System*. Glencoe, Illinois: Free Press.

Parsons, Talcott (1954). *Essays in Sociological Theory*. Glencoe, Illinois: Free Press.

Parsons, Talcott (1977). *Social Systems and the Evolutions of Action Theory*. New York: Free Press.

Patterson, Orlando (1982). *Slavery and Social Death: A Comparative Study*. Cambridge, Massachusetts: Harvard University Press.

Peach, C. (1968) *West Indian Migration to Britain*: A Social Geography. London: Oxford University Press.

Peach, C. (Ed.) (1996a) *The Ethnic Minority Populations of Great Britain*: Volume 2 of the Ethnicity in the 1991 Census. Office for National Statistics. London: HMSO.

Peach, C. (1998) South Asian and Caribbean Housing Choice in Britain. *Urban Studies*, (35) 10: 1657–1680.

Perry, T., and Delpit L. (1998). *The Real Ebonics Debates: Power, Language and the Education of African-America Children*: Boston: Beacon.

Phillips, U.B. (1918). *American Negro Slavery: A survey of the Supply, Employment, and Control of Negro Labor as Determined by the Plantation Regime*. New York: D. Appleton and Company.

Phillips, U.B. (1963). *Life and Labor in the Old South*. Boston: Little Brown.

Plowden Report (1967) Children and their Primary Schools: A report of the Central Advisory Committee on Education (England), London: HMSO.

Polanyi, Karl (2001 [1944]). *The Great Transformation: The Political and Economic Origins of Our Time*. Boston: Beacon Press.

Pollard, V. (1994). *Dread Talk: The Language of Rastafari*. Barbados, Jamaica, Trindad and Tobago: Canoe Press.

Pollard, V. (1999). Beyond Grammar: Teaching English in an Anglophone Creole Environment. In J. Rickford and S. Romaine (Eds.), *Creole Genesis, Attitudes and Discourse*. Amsterdam: John Benjamins.

Pollard, V. (2003). *From Jamaican Creole to Standard English*. Mona, Kingston. The University of the West Indies Press.

Power, S., Edwards, T., Whitty, G. & Wigfall, V. (2003) *Education and the Middle Class* Buckingham, Milton Keynes: Open University Press.

Pratt-Adams, S. Maguire, M. & Burn, E. (2010) *Changing Urban Education*. London & New York: Continuum.

Pryce, K (1979) *Endless Pressure*. Harmondsworth: Penguin.

Psathas, George (1989). *Phenomenology and Sociology: Theory and Research*. Washington, D.C.: University Press of America.

Pupil Level Annual Schools Census (PLASC). (2003). http://www.standards.dfes.gov.uk/ethnicminorities/raising_achievement/whats_new/763745/.

Rampersad, Arnold (1976). *The Art and Imagination of W.E.B. Du Bois*. Cambridge, Massachusetts: Harvard University Press.

Rampton, A. (1981) *West Indian Children in Our Schools*. Interim Report of the Committee of Inquiry into the Education of Children from Ethnic Minority Groups. London: HMSO.

Rampton, B. (1995). *Crossings: Language and Ethnicity among Adolescents*. London: Longman.

Rao, Hayagreeva et al (2005). "Border Crossing: Bricolage and the Erosion of Categorical Boundaries in French Gastronomy," *American Sociological Review* 70: 968–991.

Reed, Adolph L. (1997). *W.E.B. Du Bois and American Political Thought: Fabianism and the Color Line*. New York and Oxford: Oxford University Press.

Reyna, Stephen P. (1997). "Theory in Anthropology in the Nineties," *Cultural Dynamics* 9 (3): 325–350.

Rex, J. & Moore, R. (1967) *Race, Community & Conflict*. London: Oxford University Press.

Roediger, David R. (1999). *The Wages of Whiteness: Race and the Making of the American Working Class*. London and New York: Verso.

Rollock, N. The Black Middle Class: A Contradiction in Terms? Seminar Presentation for the 'Race' and Education: Identities and Attitudes : British Education Research Association (BERA) 'Race,' Ethnicity and Education Special Interest Group.

Roberts, P. (2007). *West Indians and their Language*. Cambridge: Cambridge University Press.

Rose, Sonya O. (1997). "Class Formation and the Quintessential Worker." In John R. Hall (Ed.), *Reworking Class* (pp. 133–166). Ithaca and London: Cornell University Press.

Rosen, H., and Burgess T. (1980). *Language and Dialects of London School Children*. London: Ward, Lock Educational.

Rosenau, Pauline Marie (1992). *Post-Modernism and the Social Sciences: Insights, Inroads, and Intrusions*. Princeton, New Jersey: Princeton University Press.

Rubin, Vera (Ed.) (1960). *Caribbean Studies: A Symposium*. Seattle: University of Washington Press.

Sahlins, Marshall (1995a). *How "Natives" Think: About Captain Cook, For Example*. Chicago: University of Chicago Press.

Sahlins, Marshall (1995b). *Historical Metaphors and Mythical Realities*. Ann Arbor: University of Michigan Press.

Sahlins, Marshall (1990). "The Political Economy of Grandeur in Hawaii from 1810–1830." In Emiko Ohnuki-Tierney (Ed.), *Culture through Time: Anthropological Approaches* (pp. 26–56). California: Stanford University Press.

Sahlins, Marshall (1989). "Captain Cook at Hawaii," *The Journal of the Polynesian Society* 98; 4: 371–423.

Sahlins, Marshall (1985). *Islands of History*. Chicago: University of Chicago Press.

Sahlins, Marshall (1982). "The Apotheosis of Captain Cook." In Michel Izard and Pierre Smith (Eds.), *Between Belief and Transgression* (pp. 73–102). Chicago: University of Chicago Press.

Sahlins, Marshall (1976). *Culture and Practical Reason*. Chicago, IL: University of Chicago Press.

Said, Edward (1979). *Orientalism.* New York: Vintage Books.

Sarup, Madan (1993). *An Introductory Guide to Post-Structuralism and Postmodernism* (second edition). Athens: The University of Georgia Press.

Saussure de, Ferdinand (1972 [1916]. *Course in General Linguistics,* Edited by Charles Bally et al. Illinois: Open Court.

Schutz, Alfred (1978). "Phenomenology and the Social Sciences." In Thomas Luckmann (Ed.), *Phenomenology and Sociology: Selected Readings* (pp. 119–141). New York: Penguin Books.

Schutz, Alfred (1978). " Some Structures of the Life-World." In Thomas Luckmann (Ed.), *Phenomenology and Sociology: Selected Readings* (pp. 257–274). New York: Penguin Books.

Schwalbe, Michael L. (1993). "Goffman Against Postmodernism: Emotion and the Reality of the Self." *Symbolic Interaction* 16(4): 333–350.

Searle, John R. (1997). *The Mystery of Consciousness.* New York: The New York Review of Books.

Sebba, M. (1993). *London Jamaican.* London: Longman.

Sebba, M. (2007) *Caribbean Creoles and Black English.* In D. Britain (Ed.) *Languages in the British Isles: Language in the British Isles.* (pp. 276–292). Cambridge: Cambridge University Press.

Sennett, Richard (1998). *The Corrosion of Character.* New York: W.W. Norton & Company.

Sewell, T. (1997) *Black Masculinity and Schooling, How Black Boys Survive Modern Schooling:* Stoke-on-Trent: Trentham Books.

Sewell, T. (2000) Identifying the Pastoral Needs of African Caribbean Students: Case of 'Critical antiracism.' Education and Social Justice, 3 (1), 17–26.

Sewell, T. & Majors, R. (2001) Black Boys and Schooling: An Intervention Framework for Understanding the Dilemmas of Masculinity, Identity and Underachievement. In R. Majors (Ed.) *Educating our Black Children: New Directions and Radical Approaches.* (pp.183–202). London: Routledge Falmer.

Shealey, M. (2006). The Promises and Perils of "scientifically based" Research for Urban Schools. *Urban Education* 4 (1): 5–19.

Shields, K. (1989). Standard English in Jamaica: A case of Competing Models. *English Worldwide* 10 (1): 41–53.

Shields, K. (1992). The Folk Come of Age: Variation and Change in Language on Air in Jamaica'. Presentation to the Association for Commonwealth Literature and Language Studies, Mona, Jamaica.

Shields, K. (1997). Requiem for English in an English-speaking community. In F.W. Schneider (Ed.), *Englishes around the World.* Amsterdam: John Benjamins.

Shields, K. (1999) Hens can crow too: The female voice of authority on air in Jamaica. In P. Christie, B. Lalla, V. Pollard, D. Carrington (Eds.). *Studies in Caribbean Language II* (pp. 187–203). St. Augustine: Studies in Caribbean Language.

Shields, K. (2002). Crowing hens are not aberrant: Gender, Culture and Performance Conversation. In P. Mohammed (Ed.), *Gendered Realities.* Mona, Kingston: University of the West Indies Press.

Siegel, J. (1999). Creole and Minority Dialects in Education: An overview. *Journal of Multingual and Multicultural Development* 20 (6): 508–531.

Siegel, J. (2007). Creole and Minority Dialects in Education: An update Language and Education. *Language and Education* 21 (1): 66–86.

Simpson, L. (2004) Statistics of Racial Segregation: measures, Evidence and Policy. *Urban Studies,* 41 (3): pp.661–681.

Sklair, Leslie (1995). *Sociology of the Global System.* Baltimore: Westview Press.

Skorupski, John (1993). *A History of Western Philosophy: English-Language Philosophy 1750–1945.* Oxford: Oxford University Press.

Slemon, Stephen (1995). "The Scramble for Post-colonialism." In Bill Ashcroft et al (Eds.), *The Post-colonial Studies Reader* (pp. 45–52). London and New York: Routledge.

Smawfield, D. (1990) Education in the British Virgin Islands: Case Study of a Caribbean Micro State. In C. Brock & D. Clarkson (Eds.), *Education in Central America and the Caribbean* (pp.138–173). London: Routledge.

Smedley, Audrey (1999). *Race in North America: Origin and Evolution of a Worldview* (Second edition). Boulder, Colorado: Westview Press.

Smiley Group, Inc. (2006). *The Covenant with Black America.* Chicago: Third World Press.

Smith M.G. (1960). "The African Heritage in the Caribbean." In Vera Rubin (Ed.), *Caribbean Studies: A Symposium* (pp. 34–46). Seattle: University of Washington Press.

Solomon, Robert C. (1988). *A History of Western Philosophy: Continental Philosophy Since 1750, The Rise and Fall of the Self.* Oxford: Oxford University Press.

Sooben, Philip, N. (1990) *The Origins of the Race Relations Act: Research Paper in Ethnic Relations* No 12. Centre for Research in Ethnic Relations. University of Warwick. web.warwick.ac.uk/fac/soc/CREC_RC/.../pdfs/...RP%20No.12.pdf. Accessed Wednesday April 18 2012.

Sowell, Thomas (1975). *Race and Economics.* New York: David McKay.

Sowell, Thomas (1981). *Ethnic America.* New York: Basic Books.

Spivak, Chakravorty Gayatri (1994 [1988]). "Can the Subaltern Speak?" In Patrick Williams and Laura Chrisma (Eds.), *Colonial Discourse and Post-Colonial Theory A Reader* (pp. 66–111). New York: Columbia University Press.

Stack, Carol B. (1974). *All Our Kin: Strategies for Survival in a Black Community.* New York: Harper & Row Publishers.

Stampp, Kenneth (1967). *The Peculiar Institution.* New York: Alfred Knopf, Inc.

Strand, S. (2012) The White British-Black Caribbean Achievement Gap: Tests, Tiers and Teacher Expectations. *British Educational Research Journal* 28 (1): pp. 75–101.

Staples, Robert (ed.) (1978). *The Black Family: Essays and Studies.* California: Wadsworth Publishing Company.

Stewart, David and Algis Mickunas (1990). *Exploring Phenomenology: A Guide to the Field and its Literature* (Second edition). Athens: Ohio University Press.

Strauss, Claudia and Naomi Quinn (1997). *A Cognitive Theory of Cultural Meaning.* United Kingdom: Cambridge University Press.

Stone, M. (1981) *Education and the Black Child: the Myth of Multicultural Education.* London: Fontana.

Stuckey, Sterling (1987). *Slave Culture: Nationalist Theory and the Foundations of Black America.* New York and Oxford: Oxford University Press.

Sturrock, John (ed.) (1979). *Structuralism and Since: From Lévi-Strauss to Derrida.* Oxford: Oxford University Press.

Sudarkasa, Niara (1980). "African and Afro-American Family Structure: A Comparison," The *Black Scholar,* 11: 37–60.

Sudarkasa, Niara (1981). "Interpreting the African Heritage in Afro-American Family Organization." In Harriette P. McAdoo (Ed.), *Black Families.* California: Sage Publications.

Sundquist, Eric J. (ed.) (1996). *The Oxford W.E.B. Du Bois Reader.* New York and Oxford: Oxford University Press.

Sutcliffe, D. (1992). *Systems in Black Language.* Avon, Clevedon: Multilingual Matters.

Swann Report (1985) *Education for all: Report of the Committee of Inquiry into the Education of children from Minority Ethnic Groups.* London: HMSO.

The Development of Education: National Report of Jamaica (2004) Kingston: Ministry of Education, Youth & Culture (August 15).

The Warnock Report (1978) Special Educational Needs. Report of the Committee of Enquiry into the Education of Handicapped Children and Young HMSO: London. http://www.educationengland.org.uk/documents/warnock/warnock00.html Accessed on Monday September 12, 2011.

Thomas, Nicholas (1982). "A Cultural Appropriation of History? Sahlins Among the Hawaiians," *Canberra Anthropology* 5; 1: 60–65.

Thompson, E.P. (1964). *The Making of the English Working Class.* New York: Pantheon Books.

Thompson, E.P. (1978). *The Poverty of Theory and Other Essays*. New York: Monthly Review Press.

Tikly, L. and Caballero, C. (2006). The Barriers to Achievement for White/Black Caribbean Students in English Schools. *British Journal of Sociology* 27(5): 569–583.

Tomlin, C. (1988). "Black Preaching Style". MPhil thesis. University of Birmingham, Birmingham.

Tomlin, C. (1999). *Black Language Style in Sacred and Secular Contexts*. Medgar Evers College (CUNY): Caribbean Diaspora Press.

Tomlinson, S. (1984) *Home and School in Multicultural Britain*. London: Batsford.

Tomlinson, S. (2001) Education in a Post-welfare Society. Buckingham: Open University Press.

Tomlinson, S. (2008) *Race & Education: Policy & Politics in Britain*. Maidenhead, Berkshire: Open University Press.

Tomlinson, S. (2011) More Radical Reform (but don't mention race) Gaps and Silences in the Government's Discourse. *Race Equality Teaching* 29 (2): 25–29.

Townsend, H.E.R. (1971) Immigrants in England: The LEA Response: Slough: National Foundation for Educational Research.

Troyna, B. (1979) Differential Commitment to Ethnic Identity by Black Youths in Britain. *New Community* (7): 406–414.

Troyna, B. (1993) *Racism and Education: Research Perspectives*. Buckingham: Open University Press.

Troyna, B. Smith, D.I. (Eds.) (1983) *Racism, School and the Labor Market*. Leicester: National Youth Bureau.

Troyna, B. and Carrington, B. (1990) *Education, Racism and Reform*: London: Routledge.

Trudgill, P. (1990). *Sociolinguistics: An Introduction*. Harmondsworth: Penguin.

Tulloch, Hugh (1999). *The Debate on the American Civil War Era*. Manchester: Manchester University Press.

Turner, Ralph H. (1976). "The Real Self: From Institution to Impulse." *American Journal of Sociology* 81: 989–1016.

Turner, Ralph H. (1988). "Personality in Society: Social Psychology's Contribution to Sociology." *Social Psychology Quarterly* 51; 1: 1–10.

Tussman, Joseph and Jacobus TenBroek (1949). "The Equal Protection of the Laws." *California Law Review* 37;3:341–381.

Wallerstein, Immanuel (1982). "The Rise and Future Demise of the World Capitalist System: Concepts for Comparative Analysis." In Hamza Alavi and Teodor Shanin (Eds.), *Introduction to the Sociology of "Developing Societies"* (pp. 29–53). New York: Monthly Review Press.

Walvin, J. (1984) Passage to Britain. Harmondsworth: Penguin.

Walvin, J. (1982) Black Ivory: A History of British Slavery. London: Harper Collins.

Ward, Glenn (1997). *Postmodernism*. London: Hodder & Stoughton Ltd.

Warren, S. and Gillborn, D. (2003). *Race Equality and Education in Birmingham*. London: Education Policy Research Unit, Institute of Education.

Watkins, S. Craig (1998). *Representing: Hip-Hop Culture and the Production of Black Cinema*. Chicago: The University of Chicago Press.

Weber, Max (1958 [1904–1905]). *The Protestant Ethic and the Spirit of Capitalism* (Talcott Parsons, Trans.). New York: Charles Scribner's Sons.

Weinreich, U. (1968). *Language in Contact*. The Hague: Mouton.

Wells, J. (1973) *Jamaican Pronunciation in London*. Oxford: Blackwell.

West, Cornel (1993). *Race Matters*. New York: Vintage Books.

West, David (1996). *An Introduction to Continental Philosophy*. Cambridge: Polity Press.

Whipple, Mark (2005). "The Dewey-Lippmann Debate Today, Communication Distortions, Reflective Agency, and Participatory Democracy." *Sociological Theory*, 23 (2): 156–178.

Williams, Raymond (1977). *Marxism and Literature*. Oxford: Oxford University Press.

Wilson, Kirt H. (1999). "Towards a Discursive Theory of Racial Identity: The Souls of Black Folk as a Response to Nineteenth-Century Biological Determinism." *Western Journal of Communication*, 63 (2): 193–215.

Wilson, William J. (1978). *The Declining Significance of Race: Blacks and Changing American Institutions*. Chicago and London: The University of Chicago Press.

Wilson, William J. (1987). *The Truly Disadvantaged*. Chicago and London: University of Chicago Press.

Winant, Howard (2001). *The World is a Ghetto: Race and Democracy since World War II*. New York: Basic Books.

Winford, D. (1993). *Predication in Caribbean Creoles*. Amsterdam: John Benjamins.

Wittgenstein, Ludwig (2001 [1953]). *Philosophical Investigations* (G.E.M. Anscombe Trans.). Malden, Massachusetts: Blackwell Publishers Ltd.

Wright, C., Weeks, D., McGlaughlin, A. & Webb, D. (eds.) (2000*) Race, Class and Gender in Exclusion from School*. London and New York: Falmer Press.

Wright, Kai (Ed.) (2001). *The African-American Archive: The History of the Black Experience in Documents*. New York: Black Dog & Leventhal Publishers.

Woodson, Carter G. (1969 [1933]). *The Mis-Education of the Negro*. Washington: Associated Publishers Inc.

Youdell, D. (2003) Identity Traps or How Black Students Fail: The Interaction Between Biographical, Sub-cultural and Learner Identities. *British Journal of Sociology of Education* 24 (1): 3–20.

Young, Iris Marion (1994). "Gender as Seriality: Thinking about Women as a Social Collective," *Signs* 19: 713–738.

Zamir, Shamoon (1995). *Dark Voices: W.E.B. Du Bois and American Thought, 1888–1903*. Chicago & London: The University of Chicago Press.

Zeitlin, Irving M. (1990). *Ideology and the development of sociological theory* (4th ed.). Englewood Cliffs, New Jersey: Prentice–Hall.

Index

www.ingramcontent.com/pod-product-compliance
Lightning Source LLC
Chambersburg PA
CBHW030655270326
41929CB00007B/377